Critical acclaim for Alice Walker

'One of the most gifted writers in her country' Isabel Allende

'One of those few writers of fiction concerning whom comparisons are immaterial. She is truly herself, and a truly wonderful writer'
Allan Massie

'Alice Walker is the brightest star in a galaxy of black American women writers' *The Times*

'This legendary writer, who with her pen has changed lives and moved minds across national, racial and sexual boundaries' *Pride*

'As a fighter against social injustice Walker is inspirational; as a black woman struggling with divorce, motherhood and catboxes, she is engaging and empathetic' *Daily Telegraph*

'[Alice Walker's] delight in life, her exuberant love of anecdote and friendship shine through . . . she is uniquely herself, as a writer of moving and transforming stories' *Observer*

'Walker's mature writing has the assurance of a woman who has confronted her demons and reached an equilibrium, without losing the fire and passion of her earlier work' *Sunday Times*

'Alice Walker is surely one of the strongest, most interesting and intelligent writers around' *San Francisco Chronicle*

Alice Walker won the Pulitzer Prize and the American Book Award for her novel *The Color Purple*. Her other bestselling novels include *By the Light of My Father's Smile*, *Possessing the Secret of Joy* and *The Temple of My Familiar*. She is also the author of several collections of short stories, essays and poetry, as well as children's books. Her books have been translated into more than two dozen languages. Born in Eatonton, Georgia, Alice Walker now lives in northern California.

BY ALICE WALKER

Fiction

The Third Life of Grange Copeland
Meridian
The Color Purple
Possessing the Secret of Joy
You Can't Keep a Good Woman Down
In Love and Trouble
The Temple of My Familiar
The Complete Stories
By the Light of My Father's Smile
The Way Forward is with a Broken Heart
Now is the Time to Open Your Heart

Poetry

Horses Make a Landscape Look More Beautiful
Once
Good Night, Willie Lee, I'll See You in the Morning
Revolutionary Petunias and Other Poems
Her Blue Body Everything We Know
A Poem Travelled Down My Arm
Absolute Trust in the Goodness of the Earth

Essays

In Search of Our Mothers' Gardens
Living by the Word
Anything We Love Can Be Saved
Sent by Earth: A Message from the Grandmother Spirit
Warrior Marks (*with Pratibha Parmar*)
The Same River Twice: Honoring the Difficult

Living by the Word

SELECTED WRITINGS 1973–1987

ALICE WALKER

PHOENIX

A PHOENIX PAPERBACK

First published in the United States of America in 1988
by Harcourt Brace Jovanovich Inc.
First published in Great Britain in 1988
by The Women's Press
This paperback edition published in 2005
by Phoenix,
an imprint of Orion Books Ltd,
Orion House, 5 Upper St Martin's Lane,
London WC2H 9EA

1 3 5 7 9 10 8 6 4 2

A CIP catalogue record for this book
is available from the British Library.

ISBN 0 75381 958 9

Printed and bound in Great Britain by
Clays Ltd, St Ives plc

www.orionbooks.co.uk

The victory belongs to love.

—*Daniel Ortega*

The teachers told us quietly that the way of experts had become a tricky way. They told us it would always be fatal to our arts to mis-use the skills we had learned. The skills themselves were mere light shells, needing to be filled out with substance coming from our souls. They warned us never to turn these skills to the service of things separate from the way. This would be the most difficult thing, for we would learn, they told us, that no fundi could work effectively when torn away from power, and yet power in these times lived far, immeasurably far from the way. This distance from the seats of power to the way, this distance now separating our way from power usurped against our people and our way, this distance would be the measure of the fundi's pain. They told us there was no life sweeter than that of the fundi in the bosom of his people if his people knew their way. But the life of a fundi whose people have lost their way is pain. All the excellence of such a fundi's craft is turned to trash. His skills are useless in the face of his people's destruction, and it is as easy as slipping on a riverstone to see his craftsmanship actually turned like a weapon against his people.

. . . Our way, the way, is not a random path. Our way begins from coherent understanding. It is a way that aims at preserving knowledge of who we are, knowledge of the best way we have found to relate each to each, each to all, ourselves to other peoples, all to our surroundings. If our individual lives have a worthwhile aim, that aim should be a purpose inseparable from the way.

. . . Our way is reciprocity. The way is wholeness.

—Ayi Kwei Armah,
TWO THOUSAND SEASONS

Contents

PREFACE

. . . .

This book was written during a period when I was not aware I was writing a book. Indeed, what I thought I had taught myself while writing *The Color Purple*, a novel, was that writing itself was no longer necessary. For years I'd longed to be alone in the middle of fields and forests, silent, without need of words. Knowing how ecstatic I can be simply lying on a hillside in the sun, I realized I will probably be happiest—anticipating all of my possible incarnations—as a blade of grass. Besides, the daily news of death and despair coming in newspapers and over the airwaves began to seem the very breath of the planet itself: ominous and foul. I started to wonder if the old planet onto which I had been born, and on which I had toddled so delight-edly as a baby, and explored so appreciatively as a child—the planet of enormous trees and mellow suns; the planet of week-long days—still existed. If it did exist, then I wanted to be reconnected with it more than I wanted anything else in life. I wanted to tell it how much I loved it, before it was too late.

I set out on a journey to find my old planet: to gaze at its moon, to swim in its waters, to eat its fruits, to rediscover and admire its creatures; to purify myself in its wind and its sun. To my inexpressible joy I found it still there, though battered as an unwanted dog. But still beautiful, still mysterious, still with week-long days (if you turn off TV and radio for months on end), still profound. Still a co*conspirator* (from the Latin *conspirare*, i.e., to breathe together). I saw, however, that it cannot tolerate much longer the old ways of humans that batter it so unmercifully, and I spent many hours and days considering how it must be possible to exist, for the good of all, in what I believe is a new age of heightened global consciousness. For in my travels I found many people sitting still and thinking thoughts similar to my own. In this study I was taught by these other people, by the art and the history of past cultures, by the elements, and by the trees, the flowers, and, most especially, the animals.

This book, give or take a few of its pieces (I was distracted along the way by this or that thrilling event, challenge, or adventure, which I was also moved to record), is a map of my journey and my discoveries.

I wish to thank my friend Susan Kirschner and my editor, John Ferrone, for their patient and thoughtful work in organizing the collection. I thank Susan especially for lobbying for the present title. I wish to thank Rebecca Walker and Robert Allen for so often being my intrepid companions; without their love always beaming in my direction I know I would have lacked a lot of the light I needed to see by. I thank Belvie Rooks for sharing adventures and work with humor and common sense. I thank my friends in Mendocino for sharing sweats, lunar eclipses, food, dance, and music, flower gardens and serpent paths and home remedies for global ills of all kinds with me. I thank Quincy Jones for the music of his being, some of which informs the wandering trails of this book. I thank Karen Vogel and Vicki Noble for The Motherpeace Tarot Deck, a constant mirror through these years. I thank all my teachers, ancestors, and spirits, especially those who have recently shifted to a different reality: the great Chinese writer Ding Ling, the great African writer Bessie Head, and the great Native American activist Billy Joe Wahpepah. I thank Bob Marley, Winnie Mandela, and Nelson Mandela for the inestimable gift of their example. I thank creation for the optimism of my spirit.

· · · · · · · · ·

JOURNAL

April 17, 1984

The universe sends me fabulous dreams! Early this morning I dreamed of a two-headed woman. Literally. A wise woman. Stout, graying, caramel-colored, with blue-gray eyes, wearing a blue flowered dress. Who was giving advice to people. Some white people, too, I think. Her knowledge was for everyone and it was all striking. While one head talked, the other seemed to doze. I was so astonished! For what I realized in the dream is that two-headedness was at one time an actual physical condition and that two-headed people were considered wise. Perhaps this accounts for the adage "Two heads are better than one." What I think this means is that two-headed people, like blacks, lesbians, Indians, "witches," have been suppressed, and, in their case, suppressed out of existence. Their very appearance had made them "abnormal" and therefore subject to extermination. For surely two-headed people have existed. And it is only among blacks (to my knowledge) that a trace of their existence is left in the language. Rootworkers, healers, wise people with "second sight" are called "two-headed" people.

This two-headed woman was amazing. I asked whether the world would survive, and she said, No; and her expression seemed to say, The way it is going there's no need for it to. When I asked her what I/we could/should do, she took up her walking stick and walked expressively and purposefully across the room. Dipping a bit from side to side.

She said: Live by the Word and keep walking.

AM I BLUE?

"Ain't these tears in these

eyes tellin' you?"*

For about three years my companion and I rented a small house in the country that stood on the edge of a large meadow that appeared to run from the end of our deck straight into the mountains. The mountains, however, were quite far away, and between us and them there was, in fact, a town. It was one of the many pleasant aspects of the house that you never really were aware of this.

It was a house of many windows, low, wide, nearly floor to ceiling in the living room, which faced the meadow, and it was from one of these that I first saw our closest neighbor, a large white horse, cropping grass, flipping its mane, and ambling about—not over the entire meadow, which stretched well out of sight of the house, but over the five or so fenced-in acres that were next to the twenty-odd that we had rented. I soon learned that the horse, whose name was Blue, belonged to a man who lived in another town, but was boarded by our neighbors next door. Occasionally, one of the children, usually a stocky teen-ager, but sometimes a much younger girl or boy, could be seen riding Blue. They would appear in the meadow, climb up on his back, ride furiously for ten or fifteen minutes, then get off, slap Blue on the flanks, and not be seen again for a month or more.

There were many apple trees in our yard, and one by the fence that Blue could almost reach. We were soon in the habit of feeding him apples, which he relished, especially because by the middle of summer the meadow grasses—so green and succulent since January—had dried out from lack of rain, and Blue stumbled about munching the dried stalks half-heartedly. Sometimes he would stand very still just by the apple tree, and when one of us came out he would whinny, snort loudly, or stamp the ground. This meant, of course: I want an apple.

It was quite wonderful to pick a few apples, or collect those that had fallen to the ground overnight, and patiently hold them, one by one, up to his large, toothy mouth. I remained as thrilled as a child by his flexible dark lips, huge, cubelike teeth that crunched the apples, core and all, with such finality, and his high, broad-breasted *enormity*; beside which, I felt small indeed. When I was a child, I used to ride horses, and was especially friendly with one named Nan until the day I was riding and my brother deliberately spooked her and I was thrown, head first, against the trunk of a tree. When I came to, I was in bed and my mother was bending worriedly over me; we silently agreed that perhaps horseback riding was not the safest sport for me. Since then I have walked, and prefer walking to horseback riding—but I had forgotten the depth of feeling one could see in horses' eyes.

4

I was therefore unprepared for the expression in Blue's. Blue was lonely. Blue was horribly lonely and bored. I was not shocked that this should be the case; five acres to tramp by yourself, endlessly, even in the most beautiful of meadows— and his was—cannot provide many interesting events, and once rainy season turned to dry that was about it. No, I was shocked that I had forgotten that human animals and nonhuman animals can communicate quite well; if we are brought up around animals as children we take this for granted. By the time we are adults we no longer remember. However, the animals have not changed. They are in fact *completed* creations (at least they seem to be, so much more than we) who are not likely *to* change; it is their nature to express themselves. What else are they going to express? And they do. And, generally speaking, they are ignored.

After giving Blue the apples, I would wander back to the house, aware that he was observing me. Were more apples not forthcoming then? Was that to be his sole entertainment for the day? My partner's small son had decided he wanted to learn how to piece a quilt; we worked in silence on our respective squares as I thought . . .

Well, about slavery: about white children, who were raised by black people, who knew their first all-accepting love from black women, and then, when they were twelve or so, were told they must "forget" the deep levels of communication between themselves and "mammy" that they knew. Later they would be able to relate quite calmly, "My old mammy was sold to another good family." "My old mammy was —— ——." Fill in the blank. Many more years later a white woman would say: "I can't understand these Negroes, these blacks. What do they want? They're so different from us."

And about the Indians, considered to be "like animals" by the "settlers" (a very benign euphemism for what they actually were), who did not understand their description as a compliment.

And about the thousands of American men who marry Japanese, Korean, Filipina, and other non-English-speaking women and of how happy they report they are, *"blissfully,"* until their brides learn to speak English, at which point the marriages tend to fall apart. What then did the men see, when they looked into the eyes of the women they married, before they could speak English? Apparently only their own reflections.

I thought of society's impatience with the young. "Why are they playing the music so loud?" Perhaps the children have listened to much of the music of oppressed people their parents danced to before they were born, with its passionate but soft cries for acceptance and love, and they have wondered why their parents failed to hear.

I do not know how long Blue had inhabited his five beautiful, boring acres before we moved into our house; a year after we had arrived—and had also traveled to other valleys, other cities, other worlds—he was still there.

But then, in our second year at the house, something happened in Blue's life. One morning, looking out the window at the fog that lay like a ribbon over the meadow, I saw another horse, a brown one, at the other end of Blue's field. Blue appeared to be afraid of it, and for several days made no attempt to go near. We went away for a week. When we returned, Blue had decided to make friends and the two horses ambled or galloped along together, and Blue did not come nearly as often to the fence underneath the apple tree.

When he did, bringing his new friend with him, there was a different look in his eyes. A look of independence, of self-possession, of inalienable *horseness*. His friend eventually became pregnant. For months and months there was, it seemed to me, a mutual feeling between me and the horses of justice, of peace. I fed apples to them both. The look in Blue's eyes was one of unabashed "this is *it*ness."

It did not, however, last forever. One day, after a visit to the city, I went out to give Blue some apples. He stood waiting, or so I thought, though not beneath the tree. When I shook the tree and jumped back from the shower of apples, he made no move. I carried some over to him. He managed to half-crunch one. The rest he let fall to the ground. I dreaded looking into his eyes—because I had of course noticed that Brown, his partner, had gone—but I did look. If I had been born into slavery, and my partner had been sold or killed, my eyes would have looked like that. The children next door explained that Blue's partner had been "put with him" (the same expression that old people used, I had noticed, when speaking of an ancestor during slavery who had been impregnated by her owner) so that they could mate and she conceive. Since that was accomplished, she had been taken back by her owner, who lived somewhere else.

Will she be back? I asked.

They didn't know.

Blue was like a crazed person. Blue *was*, to me, a crazed person. He galloped furiously, as if he were being ridden, around and around his five beautiful acres. He whinnied until he couldn't. He tore at the ground with his hooves. He butted himself against his single shade tree. He looked always and always toward the road down which his partner had gone. And then, occasionally, when he came up for apples, or I took apples to him, he looked at me. It was a look so piercing, so full of grief, a look so *human*, I almost laughed (I felt too sad to cry) to think there are people who do not know that animals suffer. People like me who have forgotten, and daily forget, all that animals try to tell us. "Everything you do to us will happen to you; we are your teachers, as you are ours. We are one lesson" is essentially it, I think. There

7

are those who never once have even considered animals' rights: those who have been taught that animals actually want to be used and abused by us, as small children "love" to be frightened, or women "love" to be mutilated and raped. . . . They are the great-grandchildren of those who honestly thought, because someone taught them this: "Women can't think," and "niggers can't faint." But most disturbing of all, in Blue's large brown eyes was a new look, more painful than the look of despair: the look of disgust with human beings, with life; the look of hatred. And it was odd what the look of hatred did. It gave him, for the first time, the look of a beast. And what that meant was that he had put up a barrier within to protect himself from further violence; all the apples in the world wouldn't change that fact.

And so Blue remained, a beautiful part of our landscape, very peaceful to look at from the window, white against the grass. Once a friend came to visit and said, looking out on the soothing view: "And it *would* have to be a *white* horse; the very image of freedom." And I thought, yes, the animals are forced to become for us merely "images" of what they once so beautifully expressed. And we are used to drinking milk from containers showing "contented" cows, whose real lives we want to hear nothing about, eating eggs and drumsticks from "happy" hens, and munching hamburgers advertised by bulls of integrity who seem to command their fate.

As we talked of freedom and justice one day for all, we sat down to steaks. I am eating misery, I thought, as I took the first bite. And spit it out.

1986

FATHER

Though it is more difficult to write about my father than about my mother, since I spent less time with him and knew him less well, it is equally as liberating. Partly this is because writing about people helps us to understand them, and understanding them helps us to accept them as part of ourselves. Since I share so many of my father's characteristics, physical and otherwise, coming to terms with what he has meant to my life is crucial to a full acceptance and love of myself.

I'm positive my father never understood why I wrote. I wonder sometimes if the appearance, in 1968, of my first book, *Once*, poems largely about my experiences in the Civil Rights movement and in other countries, notably African and Eastern European, surprised him. It is frustrating that, because he is now dead, I will never know.

In fact, what I regret most about my relationship with my father is that it did not improve until after his death. For a long time I felt so shut off from him that we were unable to talk. I hadn't the experience, as a younger woman, to ask the questions I would ask now. These days I feel we are on good terms, spiritually (my dreams of him are deeply loving and comforting ones), and that we both understand our relationship was a casualty of exhaustion and circumstances. My birth, the eighth child, unplanned, must have elicited more anxiety than joy. It hurts me to think that for both my parents, poor people, my arrival represented many more years of backbreaking and spirit-crushing toil.

I grew up to marry someone very unlike my father, as I knew him—though I feel sure he had these qualities himself as a younger man—someone warm, openly and spontaneously affectionate, who loved to talk to me about everything, including my work. I now share my life with another man who has these qualities. But I would give a lot to be able to talk grownup to grownup with Daddy. I'd like to tell him how hard I am working to understand. And about the humor and solace I occasionally find (while writing *The Color Purple*, for instance, in which some of his early life is imagined) in the work.

> My father
> (back blistered)
> beat me
> because I
> could not
> stop crying.
> He'd had
> enough "fuss"
> he said
> for one damn
> voting day.*

* From *Once* by Alice Walker. (New York: Harcourt Brace Jovanovich, Inc., 1968.)

In my heart, I have never wanted to be at odds with my father, but I have felt, over the years, especially when I was younger, that he gave me no choice. Perhaps if I could have relaxed and been content to be his favorite, there would have been a chance for closeness, but because a sister whom I loved was clearly not favorite material I did not want to be either. When I look back over my life, I see a pattern in my relationships going back to this, and in my love relationships I have refused men who loved me (at least for a time) if they in turn were loved by another woman but did not love her in return. I am the kind of woman who could positively forbid a married lover to leave his wife.

The poem above is one of my earliest as an adult, written after an abortion of which my father would not have approved, in which I felt that visceral understanding of a situation that for a poet can mean a poem. My father far away in the South, me in college in the North—how far away from each other! Yet in the pain of the moment and the illumination of some of what was wrong between us, how close. If he ever read the poem, I wonder what he thought. We never discussed my work, though I thought he tended to become more like some of my worst characters the older he got. I remember going home once and being told by my mother of some of the curses he was capable of, and hardly believing her, since the most I'd ever heard my father say was "God damn!" and I could count the number of times on toes and fingers. (In fact, his favorite curse, when a nail refused to go in straight or he dropped the hammer on his sore corn was "God damn the goddam luck to the devil!" which always sounded rather ineffectual and humorous to me, and which, thinking of it, I hear him say and see his perspiring dark face.)

Did he actually beat me on voting day? Probably not. I suppose the illegal abortion caused me to understand what living under other people's politics can force us to do. The only time I remember his beating me was one day after he'd come home tired and hungry from the dairy (where he and my brothers milked a large herd of cows morning and afternoon), and my brother Bobby, three years older than me and a lover of chaos, and I were fighting. He had started it, of course. My mother, sick of our noise, spoke to my father about it, and without asking questions he took off his belt and flailed away, indiscriminately, at the two of us.

Why do certain things stick in the mind? I recall a scene, much earlier, when I was only three or so, in which my father questioned me about a fruit jar I had accidentally broken. I felt he knew I had broken it; at the same time, I couldn't be sure. Apparently breaking it was, in any event, the wrong thing to have done. I could say, Yes, I broke the jar, and risk a whipping for breaking something valuable, or, No, I did not break it, and perhaps bluff my way through.

I've never forgotten my feeling that he really wanted me to tell the truth. And because he seemed to desire it—and the moments during which he waited for my reply seemed quite out of time, so much so I can still feel them, and, as I said, I was only three, if that—I confessed. I broke the jar, I said. I think he hugged me. He probably didn't, but I still feel as if he did, so embraced did I feel by the happy relief I noted on his face and by the fact that he didn't punish me at all, but seemed, instead, pleased with me. I think it was at that moment that I resolved to take my chances with the truth, although as the years rolled on I was to break more serious things in his scheme of things than fruit jars.

It was the unfairness of the beating that keeps it fresh in my mind. (And this was thirty-seven years ago!) And my disappointment at the deterioration of my father's ethics. And yet, since I am never happy in my heart when estranged from my father, any more than I would be happy shut off from sunlight, in writing this particular poem I tried to see my father's behavior in a context larger than our personal relationship.

Actually, my father was two fathers.

To the first four of his children he was one kind of father, to the second set of four he was another kind. Whenever I talk to the elder set I am astonished at the picture they draw, for the man they describe bears little resemblance to the man I knew. For one thing, the man they knew was physically healthy, whereas the man I knew was almost always sick; not sick enough to be in bed, or perhaps he was but with so many children to feed he couldn't afford to lie down, but "dragging-around" sick, in the manner of the very poor. Overweight, high blood pressure, diabetes, or, as it was called, "sugar," rotten teeth. There are certain *facts*, however, that identify our father as the same man; one of which is that, in the 1930s, my father was one of the first black men to vote in Eatonton, Georgia, among a group of men like himself he helped organize, mainly poor share-croppers with large families, totally at the mercy of the white landlords. He voted for Roosevelt. He was one of the leading supporters of the local one-room black school, and according to everyone who knew him then, including my older brothers and sister, believed in education above all else. Years later, when I knew him, he seemed fearful of both education and politics and disappointed and resentful as well.

And why not? Though he risked his life and livelihood to vote more than once, nothing much changed in his world. Cotton prices continued low. Dairying was hard. White men and women continued to run things, badly. In his whole life my father never had a vacation. (Of course my mother had less of one: she could not even get in the car and drive off to town, as he could.) Education merely seemed to make his children more critical of him. When I went south in the mid-sixties to help register voters, I stopped by our house to say hello but never told either of my parents what I planned to do. I didn't want them to worry about my safety, and it never occurred to me that they cared much about the vote. My father was visibly ill, paranoid, complaining the whole time of my mother's religious activities (she had become a Jehovah's Witness). Then, for no apparent reason, he would come out with one of those startlingly intelligent comments about world affairs or some absolutely clear insight into the deficiencies of national leaders, and I would be reminded of the father I didn't know.

For years I have held on to another early memory of my life between the ages of two and four. Every afternoon a tired but jolly very black man came up to me with arms outstretched. I flew into them to be carried, to be hugged, to be kissed. For years I thought this black man was my father. But no. He was my oldest brother, Fred, whose memories of my father are, surprisingly, as painful as *my* memories of him, because as my father's first child, and a son, he was subjected to my father's very confused notions of what constituted behavior suitable for a male. And of course my father himself didn't really know. He was in his late teens, a child himself, when he married. His mother had been murdered, by a man who claimed to love her, when he was eleven. His father, to put it very politely, drank, and terrorized his children.

My father was so confused that when my sister Ruth appeared in the world and physically resembled his mother, and sounded like his mother, and had similar expressions, he rejected her and missed no opportunity that I ever saw to put her down. I, of course, took the side of my sister, forfeiting my chance to be my father's favorite among the second set of children, as my oldest sister, Mamie, was favorite among the first. In her case the favoritism seemed outwardly caused by her very light color, and of course she was remarkably intelligent as well.

In my case, my father seemed partial to me because of my "smartness" and forthrightness, but more obviously because of my hair, which was the longest and "best" in the family.

And yet, my father taught me two things that have been important to me: he taught me not to bother telling lies, because the listener might be delighted with the truth, and he told me never to cut my hair. Though I have tried not to lie, the sister he rejected and I loved became a beautician, and one of the first things she did—partly in defiance of him—was to cut my shoulder-blade-length hair. I did not regret it so much while in high school and college (everyone kept their hair short, it seemed), but years later, after I married, I grew it long again, almost as long as it had been when I was growing up. I'd had it relaxed to feathers. When I walked up to my father, as he was talking to a neighbor, I stooped a little and placed his hand on my head. I thought he'd be pleased. "A woman's hair is her glory," he'd always said. He paid little attention. When the black power movement arrived, with its emphasis on cropped natural hair, I did the job myself, filling the face bowl and bathroom floor with hair and shocking my husband when he arrived home.

Only recently have I come to believe he was right in wanting me to keep my hair. After years of short hair, of cutting my hair back each time it raised its head, so to speak, I have begun to feel each time as if I am mutilating my antennae (which is how Rastafarians, among others, think of hair) and attenuating my power. It seems imperative not to cut my hair anymore.

I didn't listen to my father because I assumed he meant that in the eyes of a *man*, in his eyes, a woman's hair is her glory (unfortunately, he wore his own head absolutely clean-shaven all his life); and that is probably what he did mean. But now I begin to sense something else, that there is power (would an ancient translation of glory *be* power?) in uncut hair itself. The power (and glory) perhaps of the untamed, the undomesticated; in short, the wild. A wildness about the head, as the Rastas have discovered, places us somehow in the loose and spacious freedom of Jah's universe. Hippies, of course, knew this, too.

As I write, my own hair reaches just below my ears. It is at the dangerous stage at which I usually butt my forehead against the mirror and in resignation over not knowing "what to do with it" cut it off. But this time I have thought ahead and have encased it in braids made of someone else's hair. I expect to wear them, braces for the hair, so to speak, until my own hair replaces them. Eventually I will be able, as I was when a child, to tie my hair under my chin. But mostly I would like to set it free.

My father would have loved Jesse Jackson. On the night Jesse addressed the Democratic convention I stayed close to my radio. In my backwoods cabin, linked to the world only by radio, I felt something like my father must have, since he lived most of his life before television and far from towns. He would have appreciated Jesse's oratorical gift, and, unlike some newscasters who seemed to think of it primarily as technique, he would have felt, as I did, the transformation of the spirit of the man implicit in the words he chose to say. He would have felt, as I did, that in asking for forgiveness as well as votes and for patience as well as commitment to the Democratic party, Jackson lost nothing and won almost everything: a cleared conscience and peace of mind.

My father was never able to vote for a black candidate for any national or local political office. By the time black people were running for office and occasionally winning elections, in the late sixties and early seventies, he was too sick to respond with the exhilaration he must have felt. On the night of Jackson's speech, I felt it for him; along with the grief that in neither of our lifetimes is the United States likely to choose the best leadership offered to it. This is the kind of leader, the kind of ever-growing, ever-expanding spirit *you* might have been, Daddy, I thought—and damn it, I love you for what you might have been. And thinking of you now, merging the two fathers that you were, remembering how tightly I hugged you as a small child returning home after two long months at a favorite aunt's, and with what apparent joy you lifted me beside your cheek; knowing now, at forty, what it takes out of body and spirit to go and how much more to stay, and having learned, too, by now, some of the pitiful confusions in behavior caused by ignorance and pain, I love you no less for what you were.

1984

. . . .

TRYING TO SEE MY SISTER

On June 16, 1975, two black women were hitchhiking through the small town of Lyons, Georgia. They were returning from a visit to nearby Reidsville prison, where the brother of one of them was incarcerated and ill. They had been beaten and jailed overnight by local police, who had accused them of vagrancy and public drunkenness when one of them fainted, from the heat and the effects of her low-blood-pressure medication, along the road. Now the women were tired, humiliated, and hungry, sweaty from the severe heat, and scared. They had discovered there was no bus service back to Atlanta, where they lived.

Sometime before midnight, a white man who said he was a policeman, and who sported all the regalia of a Georgia police officer, offered them a ride. While driving them to a restaurant for a bite to eat, he implied that their troubles were over. This man was not a policeman, but an insurance agent; he had a history of accosting black women; and he had called his associate on his CB radio to meet him at the restaurant to look the two women over.

After a fight with his associate at the restaurant, the insurance man, still posing as a cop, drove the two women deep into the woods, telling them he intended to have sex with both of them. When they pleaded to be let out of the car, he threatened them with the gun he carried next to him on the seat. He wanted them to "service" him, and made other gross verbal sexual assaults that thoroughly horrified and repelled the women.

As soon as he stopped the car, one of the women jumped out and ran. The man drew his gun and pointed it after her. The other woman threw her five feet two inches against the five-foot-nine, 215-pound man and struggled to take the gun. In the process of that struggle, the gun went off twice. The man was killed by two bullet shots to the head.

The women took some money from his wallet, but left his gun, and made their way, terrified, back to Atlanta. They were arrested the following day and charged with theft and murder. The woman who ran was eventually given a five-year sentence, with three and a half years on probation. The woman who saved her iife, and saved them both from rape, was given twenty-two years, later reduced to twelve.

That woman is Dessie Woods.

There is no story more moving to me personally than one in which one woman saves the life of another, and saves herself, and slays whatever dragon has appeared. And I know that, on a subconscious level, if not a conscious one, this is work black women wish they were able to do all the time. Dessie Woods is a hero. But it is her photograph, really, as much as her story that moves me. She looks exactly like some of the women I write about, in stories and poems, and, looking at her picture, I "recognize" her life. She is a very *black* black woman (as many of those in prison and those remaining in the ghetto are), with the stunned, outraged eyes of the intelligent poor. From the photograph alone one guesses she is the sole support of her children, for her neck is as stiff as her countenance is soft, as if rubbed down, burnished, blurred by the swift, unrelenting rush of irregular events. She wears a necklace that looks like a chain; and with her short hair, the deep blackness of her skin glistening from the swampy Southern heat, she easily becomes, in imagination, the first of our mothers dragged, abused and resisting, to America.

In 1976, when I lived in New York, I began to keep a file on Dessie Woods. When I moved to San Francisco in 1978, I gave it to a friend at a feminist magazine, with the hope that she would publish something about the case. Two years later, after nothing happened there, I began a second file, and eventually contacted Dessie Woods's defense committee in San Francisco. I wanted to interview Ms. Woods, I said, in order to help publicize her case. Did they think this possible? Yes, was the reply. Two journalists from Copenhagen had interviewed her recently; why not I?

I wrote to Ms. Woods at once. Six months later, having received no response, I attempted to telephone her at Hardwick prison in Hardwick, Georgia. My call was not put through. The prisoner, I was told, was not permitted to have calls. Next I called the warden's office. His secretary said I could see Ms. Woods simply by putting my name on the visitors' list and appearing at the prison during visiting hours. When were these hours? I asked, and made arrangements to take advantage of them. A week later, I was on my way to Georgia. I stopped off in Eatonton, my hometown, and called ahead to Hardwick to make sure I was still expected next day. I was told to call back in the morning, when the warden would be in. I was asked whether I was white or black.

Next morning, when I called the prison, a black woman,

her accent unmistakable, answered the phone. My name did not appear on the visitors' list, she said. Besides, she continued, Dessie Woods was very "picky" about who she wanted to see. Also, Dessie and the warden were "very close," and, in any case, Dessie was in solitary confinement and could not receive visitors.

Meanwhile, on the wall of the supermarket where I shop in San Francisco there is a large "Free Dessie Woods!" sign scrawled in black paint. And each July 4th there are protests all over the country and in Europe, and thousands of people marching, holding aloft drawings of Dessie. In solidarity with them I write congressmen, the governor of Georgia, and Rosalyn Carter, knowing the effort is futile as I make it. The news from inside Hardwick is horrifying: Dessie is forced to remain nude in an unheated cell for long periods; she is psychologically brutalized by prison officials; and, most terrifying of all, she is being forced to take a powerful tranquilizer, which also could have serious side effects, called Prolixin.

A year after this first attempt to see Dessie, I enlist the aid of a woman who knows her lawyer. Since the lawyer lives in Chicago and rarely gets to Georgia, I agree to go for him, as his paralegal, to collect information from Dessie about her upcoming appearance before the prison parole board. He calls the prison this time, informs the officials I'm coming, and, in a matter of days, I am once again in the air.

On my way to Hardwick I stop in Atlanta to address members of the Georgia Alliance for Prison Alternatives. These are all strongly committed movement-oriented folk who are opposing the construction of a new $16,000,000 prison for women in the state of Georgia. I discover, to my horror, that seventy percent of all imprisoned women are black (and that one out of every four black men is in prison). The women are usually imprisoned for petty, even pathetic crimes: for stealing food or clothing or school supplies for their children, or for cashing continually bouncing checks, which they use to buy groceries. One woman, I am told, was imprisoned for stealing a can of Vienna sausage.

The Georgia Alliance considers it a waste of taxpayers' money to build a new prison to hold the women hit hardest by the country's economic decline. It proposes day fines or community service in place of imprisonment, thus permitting women to remain with their children, who otherwise become burdens on their relatives or on the state. Near the end of the session a woman comes forward to speak of the missing and murdered black children of Atlanta. She says that many of the children have no one to look after them, and are not even missed until their bodies are found. She says one father recognized his son's sneaker on TV. I am told by another woman, who knows the family, that Dessie Woods's teen-age children live in a condemned house, in poverty, with Dessie's old and ill mother, and that Dessie's daughter frequently runs away.

Before leaving Atlanta I accept an invitation to read poetry at a halfway house for women from Hardwick. I am told the "strange" story of Linda Rogers, a twenty-six-year-old white woman who, the women believe, was murdered by the prison doctor. She was given the same "medication" regularly given to Dessie Woods, Prolixin. She died alone in her solitary-confinement cell on February 13, 1979. She was in prison for making "harassing" phone calls.

This time I do not call ahead. I drive directly to the prison, stopping in Eatonton only long enough to tell my own old and ill mother where I am going.

Years ago, in the mid-seventies, I had visited the old Hardwick prison, on the outskirts of the sedate antebellum city of Milledgeville. I had read poetry, and marveled at the staggering indifference to the outside world of many of the women. It hadn't occurred to me that they were drugged. Now, from what I have learned about Hardwick prison, I feel sure they were. It was night when I visited, and therefore I remembered little about it, except that it was ugly, worn, and very overcrowded. The new one, built to accommodate the steadily rising numbers of women imprisoned, and itself overcrowded practically from the day it opened, looks like a junior college. With soft-yellow brick buildings set on a hill far off the main road, it seems desolate if benign, and, in fact, no sign of human life can be seen until one is actually at the door.

I go in, briefcase in hand. And there she is. Not Dessie Woods, but the black woman (in prison-guard uniform, no less) in charge of turning Dessie's sisters away. She is behind the thick glass that faces me as I enter the prison. Two white women and a white man are safely behind her, working at desks. Her eyes are wary and mournful as I tell her why I have come.

She calls the warden on the intercom, briefly turning her back to me. A moment later she says: "I'm sorry, but he says your name is not on the list."

"Check again," I say. "I am here as the paralegal of Ms. Woods's attorney. He cleared my visit to his client. Tell the warden that."

Again she speaks into the intercom. Then she turns to me. "He says there's no record of anything like that," she says. "Besides, Dessie Woods is in solitary and can't see anyone."

We look at each other hard. And I "recognize" her, too. She is very black and her neck is stiff and her countenance has been softened by the blows. All day long, while her children are supported by her earnings here, she sits isolated in this tiny glass entranceway, surrounded by white people who have hired her, as they always have, to do their dirty work for them. It is no accident that she is in this prison, too.

Because it is obvious that black women do not have the

right to self-defense against racist and sexist attacks by white men, I realize I am in prison as well. In the prison visitors' book, under the date November 10, 1980, I sign my name as witness to our common oppression, and add *"Tried* to see Dessie Woods," as a witness for myself.

1980

Postscript

At the time that I wrote to Dessie Woods, the warden, Leland Linahan, was under pressure from Linda Rogers's parents about their daughter's death. In my letter to Dessie I had said I intended to try to publish my interview with her in order to bring more attention to her case. I believe the letter was confiscated, and that she never received it.

After being turned away at the prison, I called Dessie's lawyer and received this grim news: Four days before my visit, she had appeared before the prison parole board. During the proceedings, the new acting warden (Linahan was apparently removed because of the Linda Rogers controversy) became so enraged with her that he physically attacked her and had her thrown into a solitary-confinement cell.

Meanwhile, I read in the newspapers that the proposed $16,000,000 prison for women is not being built after all. Not because of protests from the Georgia Alliance or others who object to the imprisonment of poor and black women when other alternatives are available, but because wealthy white people, who would be living some distance from the facility, did not want it in their neighborhood.

Dessie Woods was released from prison on July 9, 1981.

• • • • • • • • • •

THE DUMMY IN THE WINDOW:
JOEL CHANDLER HARRIS AND
THE INVENTION OF UNCLE REMUS

[This was originally delivered as a talk at the Atlanta Historical Society in 1981.]

About three years ago I was asked to write an essay on folklore and what it had meant in my own writing and my own development. So I thought about it, and I became very depressed— depressed, because when you think of folklore in America, you have to think of Uncle Remus and you have to think of Joel Chandler Harris. Despite this, I went to the library to begin research on Harris, partly because he lived in Eatonton, Georgia, which is my hometown. I had deliberately repressed that connection; it was really too painful to think about. And as I read his letters, collected by the wife of his son, I realized that the subject was also too painful for me to write about in an essay. So the essay is still on the shelf, but I did take some notes, and I want to share those notes with you.

Joel Chandler Harris is billed as the creator of Uncle Remus. Uncle Remus told the stories of Brer Rabbit and Brer Fox, all the classic folk tales that came from Africa and that, even now in Africa, are still being told. We, too, my brothers and sisters and I, listened to those stories. But after we saw *Song of the South*, we no longer listened to them. They were killed for us. In fact, I do not remember any of my relatives ever telling any of those tales after they saw what had been done with them.

When Joel Chandler Harris was a young boy in the 1850s and 1860s, he went out to work as an apprentice for a newspaperman on the Turnwold Plantation. We knew this place when I was growing up as the Turner place. It now has a historical marker, and often, driving past it, I stop and look at the house—a nice, big, white Southern house—and at the marker, which tells how Joel Chandler Harris created Uncle Remus.

In *Life and Letters of Joel Chandler Harris*, published in 1918 by Houghton Mifflin, Harris's daughter-in-law, Julia Collier Harris, told his story. She wrote:

When the work and play of the day were ended and the glow of the lightwood knot could be seen in the negro cabins, Joel and the Turner children would steal away from the house and visit their friends in the slave quarters. Old Harbert and Uncle George Terrell were Joel's favorite companions, and from a nook in their chimney corners he listened to the legends handed down from their African ancestors — the lore of animals and birds so dear to every plantation negro. And sometimes, while the yellow yam baked in the ashes, or the hoecake browned in the shovel, the negroes would croon a camp-meeting hymn or a corn-shucking melody. The boy unconsciously absorbed their fables and their ballads, and the soft elisions of their dialect

26

and the picturesque images of their speech left an indelible imprint upon the plastic tablets of his memory.

Here, too, he heard stories of runaway slaves and "patterollers." But Joel noticed that the patrol never visited the Turner Plantation and when, during the war, vague rumors of a negro uprising began to circulate, Mr. Turner only laughed, for he claimed that "the people who treat their negroes right have nothing to fear from them."

Thus passed the months and years at Turnwold and it was during these colorful days that the creator of "Uncle Remus," of "Mingo," and "Free Joe" received those vivid and varying impressions of the old regime and of the customs of its mansions and its cabins, — pictures of a period that passed away long before he became known as the creator of types rich in humor and poetry, and redolent of the soil to which they were bound by a thousand ties of love and sorrow, of bounty and privation.

She goes on to say:

The great popular success of the legends was a matter of strange surprise to their author. [This was around 1887, after Harris had published these books, these tales, of Uncle Remus.] He said, "It was just an accident. All I did was write out and put into print the stories I had heard all my life." When asked by an interviewer if any particular negroes suggested the "quaint and philosophic character" whom he had built up into one of the monuments of modern literature, he replied, "He was not an invention of my own, but a human syndicate, I might say, of three or four old darkies whom I knew. I just walloped them together into one person and called him 'Uncle Remus.'"

The daughter-in-law also writes:

Before leaving the subject of the first volume of Uncle
Remus stories, I cannot refrain from quoting a paragraph
of the introduction in which Father touches on the prowess
of the hero Brer Rabbit, proceeding to link up his salient
characteristics with the psychology of the negro. It is in
reference to the almost invariable conquest of the fox by
the rabbit that the author says, "It needs no scientific in-
vestigation to show why he, the negro, selects as his hero
the weakest and most harmless of all animals and brings
him out victorious in contests with the bear, the wolf, and
the fox. It is not virtue that triumphs, but helplessness. It
is not malice but mischievousness. Indeed, the parallel
between the case of all animals who must, perforce, triumph
through his shrewdness and the humble condition of the
slave raconteur is not without its pathos and poetry." Fi-
nally, the reader not familiar with plantation life is coun-
seled to "imagine that the myth stories of Uncle Remus
are told night after night to a little boy by an old negro
who appears to be venerable enough to have lived during
the period which he describes — who has nothing but
pleasant memories of the discipline of slavery."

Then she goes on to say—this wife of the son of Joel
Chandler Harris: "I have been asked many times if my husband,
the eldest son of the family, was the little boy of the stories. He
was not. And strangely enough, Father never told these stories
to his own or any other children."

But the stories were wildly successful. They were in every
household, practically, across America. And Mark Twain, in
Life on the Mississippi, tells of an encounter between Harris
and a group of children:

He deeply disappointed a number of children who had flocked eagerly to get a glimpse of the illustrious sage and oracle of the nation's nurseries. They said, when they saw this man, "Why, he's white!" They were grieved about it. So, to console them, the book was brought that they might hear Uncle Remus' Tar-baby story from the lips of Uncle Remus himself, or what, in their outraged eyes, was left of him. But it turned out that he had never read aloud to people and was too shy to venture the attempt now.

I think I know why he did not read or tell these stories to his own children. I think I know why he never said them aloud to an audience. I think he understood what he was taking when he took those stories and when he created a creature to tell those stories. There are very few people who were slaves who have "nothing but pleasant memories of the discipline" of that institution. And to base the personality of the storyteller on such a preposterous foundation constituted a deception beyond Harris's attempt somehow to pass himself off as a black man. As a white man, when he opened his mouth to speak as "Uncle Remus," perhaps he felt this.

Both of my parents were excellent storytellers, and wherever we lived, no matter how poor the house, we had fireplaces and a front porch. It was around the fireplaces and on the porch that I first heard, from my parents' lips—my mother filling in my father's pauses and he filling in hers—the stories that I later learned were Uncle Remus stories.

The most famous Brer Rabbit tale is also the most enigmatic, the story of the tar baby. In order to catch Brer Rabbit, whom he wishes to eat, Brer Fox makes a sort of doll out of tar. (In Africa, the doll is made out of rubber, hot rubber.) Brer Rabbit sees this tar baby beside the road and tries to get it to speak to him. And it can't, of course. In his frustration, he hits it with his hands and feet and is soon stuck fast.

Brer Fox comes out of hiding and says, "I've got you now."

Brer Rabbit says, "Yeah, that's true." But you know Brer Rabbit is thinking all the time. When Brer Fox says perhaps he'll cook him for dinner in a big pot, Brer Rabbit breathes a sigh of relief. "That's fine," says he. "For a minute I thought you were gonna throw me in the briar patch."

Brer Fox had not thought of this. "Maybe I'll roast you on a spit," he says, thinking of dinner, but wanting it to be a dinner only he can enjoy.

"Hey, that's cool," says Brer Rabbit. "That's a lot better than being thrown in the briar patch."

What is this briar-patch business anyway? Brer Fox is thinking. "Maybe I'll make rabbit dumplings," he says, licking his chops.

"Dumplings? Delightful," says Brer Rabbit. "Just please, please, whatever you do, *don't* throw me in the briar patch."

Now we begin to suspect that Brer Fox's hatred of Brer Rabbit is greater than his hunger. It is more important to him that Brer Rabbit suffer than that he himself be satisfied. Of course, he runs and finds the nearest briar patch and flings Brer Rabbit into it. Once unstuck from the tar baby and on the ground, Brer Rabbit laughs at Brer Fox and says, "I was born and raised in the briar patch, born and raised in the briar patch." And he gets away.

No matter how many times I heard this story as a child, I always expected Brer Fox to be able to use this considerable intelligence to help himself, rather than expend all his energy trying to harm Brer Rabbit. But my parents' point, and that of the story, was: This is the nature of Brer Fox, and a smart rabbit will never forget it.

Needless to say, my parents had never read these stories

anywhere. They had come down to them orally and were passed on to their children orally. Since none of us ever read Joel Chandler Harris, we experienced his interpretation and the stories of our own folk culture in other ways.

In Eatonton, Georgia, to this day, there is a large iron rabbit on the courthouse lawn in honor of Joel Chandler Harris, creator of Uncle Remus. There is now and has been for several years an Uncle Remus museum. There was also, until a few years ago, an Uncle Remus restaurant. There used to be a dummy of a black man, an elderly, kindly, cottony-haired darkie, seated in a rocking chair in the restaurant window. In fantasy, I frequently liberated him, using Army tanks and guns.* Blacks, of course, were not allowed in this restaurant.

The second interpretation of our folklore that we experienced was the movie *Song of the South*, an animated story of Uncle Remus and the little white children to whom he told his tales. Our whole town turned out for this movie: black children and their parents in the colored section, white children and their parents in the white section. Uncle Remus in the movie saw fit largely to ignore his own children and grandchildren in order to pass on our heritage—indeed, our birthright—to patronizing white children, who seemed to regard him as a kind of talking teddy bear.

I don't know how old I was when I saw this film—probably eight or nine—but I experienced it as vastly alienating, not only from the likes of Uncle Remus—in whom I saw aspects of my father, my mother, in fact all black people I knew who told these stories—but also from the stories themselves, which, passed into the context of white people's creation, the same white people who, in my real everyday life, would not let a black

* See my short story "Elethia" in *You Can't Keep a Good Woman Down* for the creative solution to this problem.

person eat in a restaurant or through their front door, I perceived as meaningless. So there I was, at an early age, separated from my own folk culture by an invention.

I believe that the worst part of being in an oppressed culture is that the oppressive culture—primarily because it controls the production and dispersal of images in the media—can so easily make us feel ashamed of ourselves, of our sayings, our doings, and our ways. And it doesn't matter whether these sayings, doings, or ways are good or bad. What is bad about them and, therefore, worthy of shame, is that they belong to us.

Even our folklore has been ridiculed and tampered with. And this is very serious, because folklore is at the heart of self-expression and therefore at the heart of self-acceptance. It is full of the possibilities of misinterpretation, full of subtleties and danger. And in accepting one's own folklore, one risks learning almost too much about one's self. For instance, if you read these tales, you will see throughout them various things about us that we have to accept because they are true reflections, but they're painful. My view is that we needn't pull away from them because of the pain. We need simply to try to change our own feelings and our own behavior so that we don't have to burden future generations with these same afflictions. There's a lot of self-criticism in the folklore, for instance, and things that are really, sometimes, unsettling.

Joel Chandler Harris and I lived in the same town, although nearly one hundred years apart. As far as I'm concerned, he stole a good part of my heritage. How did he steal it? By making me feel ashamed of it. In creating Uncle Remus, he placed an effective barrier between me and the stories that meant so much to me, the stories that could have meant so much to all of our children, the stories that they would have heard from their own people and not from Walt Disney.

1981

LONGING TO DIE OF OLD AGE

Mrs. Mary Poole, my "4-greats" grandmother, lived the entire nineteenth century, from around 1800 to 1921, and enjoyed exceptional health. The key to good health, she taught (this woman who as an enslaved person was forced to carry two young children, on foot, from Virginia to Georgia), was never to cover up the pulse at the throat. But, with the benefit of hindsight, one must believe that for her, as for generations of people after her, in our small farming community, diet played as large a role in her longevity and her health as loose clothing and fresh air.

For what did the old ones eat?

Well, first of all, almost nothing that came from a store. As late as my own childhood, in the fifties, at Christmas we had only raisins and perhaps bananas, oranges, and a peppermint stick, broken into many pieces, a sliver for each child; and during the year, perhaps, a half-dozen apples, nuts, and a bunch of grapes. All extravagantly expensive and considered rare. You ate *all* of the apple, sometimes, even, the seeds. Everyone had a vegetable garden; a garden as large as there was energy to work it. In these gardens people raised an abundance of food: corn, tomatoes, okra, peas and beans, squash, peppers, which they ate in summer and canned for winter. There was no chemical fertilizer. No one could have afforded it, had it existed, and there was no need for it. From the cows and pigs and goats, horses, mules, and fowl that people also raised, there was always ample organic manure.

Until I was grown I never heard of anyone having cancer.

In fact, at first cancer seemed to be coming from far off. For a long time if the subject of cancer came up, you could be sure cancer itself wasn't coming any nearer than to some congested place in the North, then to Atlanta, seventy-odd miles away, then to Macon, forty miles away, then to Monticello, twenty miles away. . . . The first inhabitants of our community to die of acknowledged cancer were almost celebrities, because of this "foreign" disease. But now, twenty-odd years later, cancer has ceased to be viewed as a visitor and is feared instead as a resident. Even the children die of cancer now, which, at least in the beginning, seemed a disease of the old.

Most of the people I knew as farmers left the farms (they did not own the land and were unable to make a living working for the white people who did) to rent small apartments in the towns and cities. They ceased to have gardens, and when they did manage to grow a few things they used fertilizer from boxes and bottles, sometimes in improbable colors and consistencies, which they rightly suspected, but had no choice but to use. Gone were their chickens, cows, and pigs. Gone their organic manure.

To their credit, they questioned all that happened to them. Why must we leave the land? Why must we live in boxes with hardly enough space to breathe? (Of course, indoor plumbing seduced many a one.) Why must we buy all our food from the store? Why is the price of food so high—and it so tasteless? The collard greens bought in the supermarket, they said, "tasted like water."

The United States should have closed down and examined its every intention, institution, and law on the very first day a black woman observed that the collard greens tasted like water. Or when the first person of any color observed that store-bought tomatoes tasted more like unripened avocados than tomatoes.

The flavor of food is one of the clearest messages the Universe ever sends to human beings; and we have by now eaten poisoned warnings by the ton.

When I was a child growing up in middle Georgia in the forties and fifties, people still died of old age. Old age was actually a common cause of death. My parents inevitably visited dying persons over the long or short period of their decline; sometimes I went with them. Some years ago, as an adult, I accompanied my mother to visit a very old neighbor who was dying a few doors down the street, and though she was no longer living in the country, the country style lingered. People like my mother were visiting her constantly, bringing food, picking up and returning laundry, or simply stopping by to inquire how she was feeling and to chat. Her house, her linen, her skin all glowed with cleanliness. She lay propped against pillows so that by merely turning her head she could watch the postman approaching, friends and relatives arriving, and, most of all, the small children playing beside the street, often in her yard, the sound of their play a lively music.

Sitting in the dimly lit, spotless room, listening to the lengthy but warm-with-shared-memories silences between my mother and Mrs. Davis was extraordinarily pleasant. Her white hair gleamed against her kissable black skin, and her bed was covered with one of the most intricately patterned quilts I'd ever seen—a companion to the dozen or more she'd stored in a closet, which, when I expressed interest, she invited me to see.

I thought her dying one of the most reassuring events I'd ever witnessed. She was calm, she seemed ready, her affairs were in order. She was respected and loved. In short, Mrs. Davis was having an excellent death. A week later, when she had actually died, I felt this all the more because she had left, in me, the indelible knowledge that such a death is possible. And that cancer and nuclear annihilation are truly obscene alternatives. And surely, teaching this very vividly is one of the things an excellent death is supposed to do.

To die miserably of self-induced sickness is an aberration we take as normal; but it is crucial that we remember and teach our children that there are other ways.

For myself, for all of us, I want a death like Mrs. Davis's. One in which we will ripen and ripen further, as richly as fruit, and then fall slowly into the caring arms of our friends and other people we know. People who will remember the good days and the bad, the names of lovers and grandchildren, the time sorrow almost broke, the time loving friendship healed.

It must become a right of every person to die of old age. And if we secure this right for ourselves, we can, coincidentally, assure it for the planet. And that, as they say, will be excellence, which is, perhaps, only another name for health.

1985

· · · · · · · · ·

THE OLD ARTIST: NOTES ON MR. SWEET

[For many years after writing "To Hell with Dying" I thought
of how good it would be as a story for children, proving as it
does that imperfection is no barrier to love, one of the great
fears that children have. Alas, no appropriate illustrator could
be found. And then one day one *was* found, and the book was
published: *To Hell with Dying*, illustrations by Catherine Dee-
ter. The editor asked how the story came about.]

· · ·

I like to use the case of Mr. Sweet, in "To Hell with Dying,"
as an example of a story that is "autobiographical" (is this or
that piece autobiographical? some puzzled reader is always ask-
ing), though little of it ever happened. The *love* happened, and
that is the essence of the story.

There was, in fact, in my rural, farming, middle-Georgia

childhood, in the late forties and early fifties, an old guitar player called Mr. Sweet. If people had used his given name, he would have been called Mr. Little; obviously nobody agreed that this was accurate. Sweet was. The only distinct memory I have is of him playing his guitar while sitting in an ancient, homemade (by my grandfather) oak-bottomed chair in my grandmother's cozy kitchen while she baked biscuits and a smothered chicken. He called the guitar his "box." I must have been eight or nine at the time.

He was an extremely soulful player and singer, and his position there by the warm stove in the good-smelling kitchen, "picking his box" and singing his own blues, while we sat around him silent and entranced, seemed inevitable and right. Although this is the only memory I have of him, and it is hazy, I know that Mr. Sweet was a fixture, a rare and honored presence in our family, and we were taught to respect him—no matter that he drank, loved to gamble and shoot off his gun, and went "crazy" several times a year. He was an artist. He went deep into his own pain and brought out words and music that made us happy, made us feel empathy for anyone in trouble, made us think. We were taught to be thankful that anyone would assume this risk. That he was offered the platter of chicken and biscuits first (as if he were the preacher and even if he was tipsy) seemed only just.

Mr. Sweet died in the sixties, while I was a student at Sarah Lawrence College, in Westchester, New York, in an environment so different from the one in which he and my parents lived, and in which I had been brought up, that it might have existed on another planet. There were only three or four other black people there, and no poor people at all as far as the eye could see. For reasons not perhaps unrelated to this discrepancy, I was thinking of dying myself at the very time I got the news of his death. But something of my memory of Mr. Sweet stopped me: I remembered the magnitude of his problems—problems I was just beginning to truly understand—as a black man and as an artist, growing up poor, forced to endure the racist terrorism of the American South. He was unlucky in love, and no prince as a parent. *Irregardless*, as the old people said, and Mr. Sweet himself liked to say, not only had he lived to a ripe old age (I doubt that killing himself ever entered his head, however, since I think alcoholism was, in his case, a slow method of suicide), but he had continued to share all his troubles and his insights with anyone who would listen, taking special care to craft them for the necessary effect. *He continued to sing*.

This was obviously my legacy, as someone who also wanted to be an artist and who was not only black and poor, but a woman besides, if only I had the guts to accept it.

Turning my back on the razor blade, I went to a friend's house for the Christmas holidays (I was too poor even to consider making the trip home, a distance of about a thousand miles), and on the day of Mr. Sweet's burial I wrote "To Hell with Dying." If in my poverty I had no other freedom—not even to say good-bye to him in death—I still had the freedom to love him and the means to express it, if only to myself. I wrote the story with tears pouring down my cheeks. I was grief-stricken, I was crazed, I was fighting for my own life. I was twenty-one.

It was the first short story I ever published, though it was not the first one I wrote. The first one I wrote, before my memory of Mr. Sweet saved me ("To Hell with Dying" illustrates, I think, my wish that I could have returned the favor), was entitled "The Suicide of an American Girl."

The poet Muriel Rukeyser was my don (primary teacher) and friend at Sarah Lawrence. So was Jane Cooper, in whose writing course I wrote the story. Between them they warmly affirmed the life of Mr. Sweet and the vitality of my art, which,

I was beginning to see, merged in unexpected ways, very healing and effective ways, with my life. I was still hanging by a thread, so their enthusiasm was important. Without my knowledge, Muriel sent the story to the greatest of the old black singer poets, Langston Hughes, who loved it immediately, and said so, and who was able to publish it two years after he read it.

When I met Langston Hughes I was amazed. He was another Mr. Sweet! Aging and battered, full of pain, but writing poetry, and laughing, too, and always making other people feel better. It was as if my love for one great old man down in the poor and beautiful and simple South had magically, in the new world of college and literature and poets and publishing and New York, led me to another.

1987

MY BIG BROTHER BILL

· · · · · · · · · · · ·

[At a powwow in honor of Bill Wahpepah shortly after his death, Carol Wahpepah, his widow, asked those of us who had memories of Bill to write a collection of them for his children. This was my response to her request.]

· · ·

In regard to the contact between the two races, by which such stories (i.e., the "Uncle Remus" tales) could be borrowed from one by the other, it is not commonly known that in all the southern colonies Indian slaves were bought and sold and kept in servitude and worked in the fields side by side with negroes up to the time of the Revolution. Not to go back to the Spanish period, when such things were the order of the day, we find the Cherokee as early as 1693 complaining that their people were being kidnapped by slave hunters. Hundreds of captured Tuscarora and nearly the whole tribe of the Appalachee were distributed as slaves among the Carolina colonists in the early part of the eighteenth century, while the Natchez and others shared a similar fate in Louisiana, and as late at least as 1776 Cherokee prisoners of war were still sold to the highest bidder for the same purpose. At one time it was charged against the governor of South Carolina that he was provoking a general Indian war by his encouragement of slave hunts. Furthermore, as the coast tribes dwindled they were compelled to associate and intermarry with the negroes until they finally lost their identity and were classed with that race, so that a considerable proportion of the blood of the southern negroes is unquestionably Indian.

—James Mooney*

I first met Bill Wahpepah in the fall of 1984, in Custer, South Dakota; I think perhaps our mutual friend Belvie Rooks introduced us. She and I were in Custer to attend the trial of Dennis Banks,† and I was coming out of a long period of spiritual reassessment and political hibernation. On top of everything

* MYTHS OF THE CHEROKEE AND SACRED FORMULAS OF THE CHEROKEES, *collected and transcribed* 1887–1890. (*Nashville: Charles and Randy Elder-Booksellers, Publishers, in collaboration with Cherokee Heritage Books, Cherokee, NC, 1982*).

† "At about 10:30 Thursday morning, September 13th, 1984, Dennis Banks (American Indian Movement—AIM—leader) took a courageous step toward gaining his eventual freedom by surrendering to law enforcement officials in Rapid City, South Dakota. Banks, who fled South Dakota in 1975 because of threats against his life by William Janklow (Governor of South Dakota) and prison guards, was convicted of assault (without intent to kill) and riot. This conviction grew out of a demonstration that erupted into a riot in Custer, South Dakota on February 6th, 1973. The demonstration by approximately 150 Indian people came about because of the judicial mishandling of a case involving the death of an Indian youth at the hands of a white man. (The accused was eventually acquitted.)" From a flier prepared by Mark Banks, National Director, Dennis Banks Support Committee.

else—by which I mean the assassinations of the sixties and seventies, the repressions (on Indian reservations and in ghettos, in particular) of the seventies and eighties, and the rape and brutalization of the planet in general—the election of Ronald Reagan, with Nancy Reagan posited as a desirable model of twentieth-century womanhood, had hit me hard. During this period, which encompassed several years, Indians were very much in my consciousness. There was my mother's mostly Cherokee grandmother to contend with in myself, for instance. There was my gravitation toward Indian art and artifacts, which had in fact started years earlier: the need to have arrowheads on my person (I never flew without one) and Indian pottery, jewelry, and rugs around. And there was my study of Cherokee folklore and folkways: I made the astonishing discovery that the animal tales, commonly known in North America as "Uncle Remus" stories, which, as told by my parents, I grew up listening to as a child, and which I had assumed were from Africa, could as easily be from the Cherokee, since the very same tales abound in their folk "literature." I also discovered what appeared to me to be the origin, or one interesting possible origin, of the expression "the blues." Among the Cherokee the color blue itself was "emblematic of failure, disappointment, unsatisfied desire."* When one felt that way, one painted one's body or part of one's body blue. When one felt better, red was the color of choice. I began to recognize in the faces of the people among whom I grew up traces of the Cherokee Indian tribe that everyone around me, when I was a child, had claimed was gone forever, last seen as its members left Georgia on the ominous Trail of Tears. And of course the myth the white people perpetuated to make black people feel even worse about having been enslaved was that the Indians, warriors to the last man, had never been.

* Mooney, *Myths of the Cherokee*.

Prominent among the people I was now scrutinizing was Miss Bessie, long-haired and high-nosed, whom everyone in our community automatically called "The Indian." She was very poor, like most of us, and a great believer in sharing, but to a greater extent than even my parents, who were very generous; she would give you anything she had. You had only to admire something sincerely, a spool of thread, a plant, or a kitchen object, and it was yours. In fact, to me, Miss Bessie, still alive and nearing a hundred, remains a primary symbol of human generosity.

In my apartment I lived with Edward S. Curtis's photographs of Indians on every wall; I began to feel that the faces he photographed spoke directly to me. I studied the people's clothing, their adornments, their hair; I noticed particularly their sense of aesthetics, their sense of style. I could see that of all the clothing styles created in or imported into North America, theirs was still the most intrinsically elegant. Over a period of months I made a thorough investigation into the merits of the teepee and stopped only a little short of buying and living in one. No other structure seemed so sensible for the landscape and for the nomadic life style Indians enjoyed. I needed the reading of the folklore, I needed the photographs around me. Especially the photographs. Indians do not live in history books; every one encountered there is dead. But in the folklore Indians are still acting colored and telling jokes, and in the photographs they are still looking out at the world and at the white man with infinitely expressive faces and not managing to keep all that they are thinking to themselves. Of what devastation, to the environment and to other human beings, we are now witnessing did their incredulous expressions forewarn!

After meeting Bill Wahpepah that day in Custer, where signs of the exploitation of Indians still abound (wooden "cigar-store" Indians, fake war bonnets, and "Indian" silver-and-turquoise jewelry fill the store windows along the main street), I stood in front of the courthouse where the trial was to be held and waited for the doors to open. When they finally did open, after a very long time, the white Southern-looking and Southern-sounding officer advised us that only a fraction of the large crowd outside (several hundred women, children, and men, including three Buddhist monks—although I discovered months later that at least one of them was a woman—who were beating gongs) would be let inside. A few family members, a few of the elders, a few of the press. I was none of these. I was merely a witness, at the moment rather feeble from the blows of oppression that, in the case of the Indians, I could see were presumably unending; I was only a pair of eyes, a body, a flagging though faithful heart. But out of the crowd Big Bill appeared. He seemed enormous, and was—two hundred pounds at least—very dapper in vest, long braids, headband, and beads. And, taking me by the shoulders with his large hands, he propelled me forward until I stood in the midst of the elders, a group of ancient, intricately wrinkled Indian women, wrapped in blankets. I was remarkably content to be there, as we all settled in, huddled together, to wait.

Eventually both Belvie and I were admitted to the courtroom, but only for a short portion of the trial. No one, beyond the family, the elders, and the white men who represented the press, was to see this carriage of "justice" from start to finish. We were at least able to see Dennis and Kamook and their children, their love for one another announced in every movement of their bodies and every glance of their apprehensive eyes. Dennis was especially beautiful in a red robe, with feathers in the long braids that hung down his back and with sneakers on his feet, though his face had the haggard pallor of one whose fate has for generations rested in the hands of his enemies.

•   •   •

Shortly after the trial—Dennis had been sentenced to prison for three years—and after I had returned to San Francisco, I was asked by Bill Wahpepah to join the program of a fundraiser for the International Indian Treaty Council, of which he was director of information. One of the things the Council does is connect Indians of all continents with each other; today, because of people like Bill Wahpepah, indigenous peoples from New Zealand to Nicaragua are talking together, sharing their experiences and struggles. To my mind, this is one of the best things happening on the planet.

To his surprise, I think, I said yes. Some of Bill's style is expressed in his letter to me about the event. "Dear Alice," he wrote, "we have this idea of asking you to read with this man, John Trudell. . . ." Enclosed was a tape of John's work. An incredibly powerful and sensitive poet, whose family had been firebombed to death in retaliation for his activity in the American Indian Movement at Wounded Knee, John moved me profoundly, as did the beating of the ceremonial drum over which he read. I was delighted to read with him. On the night of the event I asked Bill if it would be appropriate for the drums to sound for me, as well. He said "sure," and invited the drummers to drum as I read. There were six of them around the large drum, and their steady, ancient drumming seemed to reawaken in me the very beat of my nearly dormant poet's heart. I knew that my spiritual reassessment had reached another plateau and that my political hibernation was over.

Bill and I were to work together several times before he died. When I learned he was not well—he spoke many times about the earlier years of his life, when the use of drugs and alcohol constituted his response to despair—I invited him and his family to visit with me in the country. Actually, that expression "to visit with" is Bill's. The first time, he came with his wife, Carol, and the boys, Renchul and Choko; the second time, he came alone. I was not there—for some reason, it was always hard to synchronize our "visiting"—but a friend who stopped by tells a lovely story of Bill blissed out, naked as a jaybird (presumably), splashing about in the pond. It was during that visit that he planted tobacco seeds in the garden, very neatly and with their own little staked fence. (They never came up; when I asked Bill about them he said he'd gotten them from some old-timer on the reservation, and, no, he had no idea why they didn't come up. He knew very little about such things, he said. We laughed at this admission.) He hung tiny "medicine bundles" of cedar, with wrappings of red flannel, from trees in the yard and over the front door. I was left also with a substantial supply of sage, some of which Bill had burned in an abalone shell, which still retained the residue. This was rather wonderful: to walk into my studio after Bill's visits and to find these unexpected gifts, not the least of which was the smell of sage smoke. I always think of the place where I work as holy; Bill seemed to sense that instinctively, and, indeed, we once had a brief conversation, if I remember correctly, in which I told him that I'd come to understand my work as prayer, and he said he understood his the same way. I always felt very comfortable talking with Bill about prayer and Mother Earth and the spirits that, if you are open to them, are ever present. He had such empathy with the suffering of the Earth, as Belvie always said, that when he spoke about her you thought it was some human being he knew.

On his last visit to the country he looked very tired and his eyes were sad. We sat on the deck above the garden, and he said a touching thing: "I want my children to continue to know you." I thought he said this because, the afternoon before, I had been out along the road and pond sowing wild-flower seeds with them, and laughing; like their father, they didn't seem to have much faith that anything was going to come up.

He said it very directly and with emphasis in his quiet voice, and I felt that he knew his health was very, very bad, and that he was making preparations to go. He also told me that Carol was a fine artist and that he regretted she hadn't had much time to do her own work, because being a mother and wife and working with the Treaty Council took up so much of her time. I hadn't known about Carol's art (beautiful sculpture and drawings); I was to see my first drawing by her on an invitation to a birthday party for Bill shortly before he died.

My mood was too peculiar the night of the party to risk inflicting it on others, and so I called and explained I couldn't come. I consoled myself by thinking about how good Bill had looked the last time I'd seen him, when he brought a woman by my house to sell me some Big Mountain Support Group Navajo/Dineh rugs. He was slimmer than usual and wore a dark shirt and trousers and a blue Greek fisherman's cap. I told him he was looking great, and he said he'd cut down on red meat. Since I think the consumption of red meat accounts for at least half of the world's ills, I was extremely happy to hear this. He told a rather bawdy joke that I didn't get, about an Indian and his saddle horn. I asked him to repeat it, and it never got any funnier; but it showed me another side of Bill that I'd never guessed.

When I heard he'd died, I didn't feel sad right away. Belvie called to tell me and there were tears in her voice. I thought about his jokes and his voice and his tobacco seeds and his commitment to being an authentic person, always willing to give full accounts of his good years and his bad, and his patience with his children. Even at his farewell ceremony, at which I thought he looked quite justified and content with himself, I cried less for him—"free at last!"—than for the rest of us. What a mess the world is in! I thought. What peace to get away! But sometime later I felt very sad, because I missed him and because people like Bill are part of the foundation that holds the whole world up. Then I heard him say: Ah, hell, let somebody else hold the damn thing up for a while, and I felt more cheerful.

He lived a good life, with suffering, struggle, joy, children, whole peoples of all continents in it. He was forever receiving energy and support and love from those who recognized his magnificence as a human being, and he was forever giving back more than he got. I was glad that my years spent locating the Indian within myself prepared me for a friendship with Bill that proceeded in love, dignity, and remarkable harmony. He used to tell me that I helped him to affirm the connection between "Indians of the Americas" and "Indians [Africans] of Africa," and we were both thrilled when the faces of Nelson Mandela and Leonard Peltier appeared together on Indian Treaty Council T-shirts and when, at rallies, their names became linked in the same breath. There were all his small but meaningful gifts of understanding; like his saying to me once, as my book *The Color Purple* was being criticized because of the character of Mister: "There's a little bit of Mister in all of us." Exactly my feeling. And, when he asked me to do a benefit for the Treaty Council and I declined, he understood when Belvie explained that it was because of the time of year. Alice is like a plant, she told him, she goes to sleep during the winter months, but she wakes up again in the spring.

Ohhhh, said Bill, imagining me, no doubt, as corn. At least I hope so.

Actually, Bill felt more like a big brother than anything else. There was a special affinity between us based on the common intuitive knowledge that, in a sense, all indigenous peoples are, by their attachment to Mother Earth and experience with Wasichus,* Conquistadors, and Afrikaners, one. I loved stand-

* A Sioux word meaning "the fat taker"—the white man.

ing on a stage next to Bill (one night in Berkeley especially comes to mind, when there were also Pete Seeger and Ogie Yocha, the radical Korean-Japanese rock-reggae band), wrapped in the red Indian shawl he gave me at one of our more amazingly soulful and festive events, as we listened to the voices and the drums of all our people, alive again.

1987

JOURNAL

August 30, 1984

Have finished a typed draft of the "Coming In from the Cold" essay. And the sun is peeking through the clouds after a rainy morning. The fire takes this same opportunity to blaze. Deer keep wandering across the yard. I went out and spoke to a couple of them. I can tell my voice doesn't frighten them. They are very hungry for green things, since all is dry and dead this time of year. Perhaps I'll pick the greens in the garden and give them those.

Joan came to fix lunch, a fairly acidic (tomatoey) soup. It was nice, though, to work, typing, while she cooked.

I'm sure I'll want to work on the essay before delivering it at the Writers Union meeting. But I'm *grateful* that it came at all. I've felt so empty, so much as if I might just dive off forever into my hollyhocks. But even though it seems like a very un-productive year, this is not true. I've managed to rest a lot, my first priority. I did finish a draft of the screenplay [of *The Color Purple*] and now this essay, as well as the introduction to California's book [*A Piece of Mine*]. And my own book will be out in October. Rebecca and I will be okay, I think. Our bond seems to have deepened over the year.

My blessings continue. Thank you.

August 31, 1984

In fact, you continue to amaze me! Yesterday after Joan arrived I went up to the studio to get tomatoes for visiting friends—there are so many, you've really outdone yourself! And when I got there I went to the outhouse, where a family of wasps now live, and then I went up the hill to the meditation yurt, stopping to lie down on the way. The view is so incredibly lovely—your work again! Indeed all around me. I never cease to marvel at how you do it—to me, everything is magic, but just from my own work experience I know the manifestation of magic is work. Or vice versa. Anyhow, went inside the clean-swept yurt and meditated. Or tried. But what happened instead is that you gave me a whole, long story called "The Hair Artist." I was astonished. And humbled and proud. I hesitate to write "proud"; I think I mean it in the sense of overjoyed, thrilled at this gift that seems to say I still know you. And you know me, in the sense of letting me feel creation along with you. So now I'm excited about the prospect of bringing it out—in fact, I was so excited, and so full of thoughts, I could hardly go to sleep. Eventually I did and I woke up this morning feeling healed; the pain in shoulder, neck, and ear, soothed. And the sun is shining and I've put a wash in the machine that shakes the house.

There is no doubt in my mind that I am blessed. That you are present in the cosmos and in me and that we are breathing together—conspiracy. I see now what is meant by faith and the giving up of the self to the spirit. I thank you for your gifts. All of them. I see you are trying to teach me all the time. I think of this when the lessons hurt. I love you.

• • • • • • • • • •

COMING IN FROM THE COLD:

WELCOMING THE OLD, FUNNY-TALKING

ANCIENT ONES INTO THE WARM ROOM

OF PRESENT CONSCIOUSNESS,

OR, NATTY DREAD RIDES AGAIN!

[I read this essay both at the National Writers Union in New York in spring of 1984 and at the Black Women's Forum in Los Angeles on November 17, 1984.]

• • •

This summer I was stricken with a severe case of what my friend Gloria Steinem calls "Hollyhockitis." This means I hounded my friends and nursery companies for hollyhock plants, was eventually sent some plants by a friend who lives in Oregon, and proceeded to tend them with assiduous attention. I've decided that some of us, fearful that the world we know might not outlive the year, the month, the moment, turn instinctively to the planting of things we especially love. Last summer it was snapdragonitis. I feel Oriental poppyitis coming on for next summer.

As I was finishing up my daily scrutiny of each hollyhock bud, which seemed in no hurry to open, my neighbor on the next ridge, a lesbian sculptor and potter of great talent, arrived on my doorstep. She had just finished the evening milking of her goats, she said, when she received a call from a feminist bookstore in San Francisco, some hundred and forty miles away; the Channel 7 News van was apparently backed up in front of their door, and the newscaster inside had informed the bookstore owners that *The Color Purple* was up for banning—because a local mother had objected to its use in the Oakland public schools—and since they sold the book, what did they think of this?

Their response was to put the newscaster on hold, call my neighbor, and ask her to tramp up the hill and down the ravine, through the trees and underbrush and sticker-briar, and across the creek to ask me what they should say. The women who own the store had sold hundreds, if not thousands, of copies of *The Color Purple*, yet they had no opinion on whether or not it should be suppressed.

What could I say about the powerlessness of such sister-hood?

I invited my neighbor to share the remains of a bottle of champagne a thoughtful house guest had left in the fridge, and we spent a pleasant half hour talking about snapdragons, holly-hocks, porcelain sculpture, and goats.

Every few days for the next couple of weeks I went down to the village and picked up a paper to see how the banning was coming along. I learned that a certain Mrs. Green had objected to having her daughter, Donna, read *The Color Purple*. In her opinion the book was too sexually explicit, presented a stereotyped view of blacks, and degraded black people by its "exposure" of their folk language.

Mrs. Green had not actually read the book, according to

the papers; she'd "flipped" through it, scanned at least five pages, photocopied those five, and passed them out to the members of the Oakland school board. One of its members, who also had not read the book, a black woman (Mrs. Green hails as white), readily agreed that the book should be banned from the school. She termed it "garbage."

Well.

For weeks the battle raged, on a number of fronts. One friend was in her car trying to listen to music when she found herself in the middle of a radio-listener poll to determine whether *The Color Purple* should be banned. The poll was conducted, she said, at eleven o'clock in the morning, when most colored folk are at work. This alone outraged her. She says she nearly ran down several leisurely moving San Francisco tourists while trying to find a telephone, and when she did, she called everyone she knew. They in turn called the radio station. How this particular poll turned out, I do not know; I heard about it considerably after the fact; however, I did notice that the impact of the controversy on book sales was immediate. For months *The Color Purple* had been the number-one trade-paperback best seller in the Bay Area, according to the local paper, the *San Francisco Chronicle*; then at one point it had slipped down as far as number three. The dispute over the possible banning brought it right back up again, with newly interested high-school students, especially in Oakland, buying heavily.

Reporters were unable to reach me. If they did get someone at my house, they were told I had severe hollyhockitis and it was contagious. I felt I had written the book as a gift to the people. All of them. If they wanted it, let them fight to keep it, as I had had to fight to deliver it. I was tired and deserved my rest. I consulted the ancestors on my position, and they agreed with me (in language that would have upset Mrs. Green).

Eventually a committee was formed to study the merits of

The Color Purple, to determine whether it was degrading to black people, repugnant to whites, and generally bad for growing minds. Meanwhile, the students, teachers, and principal of the school from which the effort to ban the book arose sent me a telegram inviting me to speak at their upcoming commencement, an invitation that moved me but which my by-now-*passionate* (the buds were opening!) hollyhockitis made easy to decline. The committee, composed of all colors and both (or more) sexes, representative of the people as only a Bay Area, California, committee can be, exonerated the book, while at the same time treating Mrs. Green and her objections with patience, understanding, tact, and even gentleness—for which I was glad.

For I feel I know what Mrs. Green was objecting to. When I learned she'd copied and distributed to the school board five pages from the book, I knew which five pages they were. They are the first five pages of the book. The same five pages *my* mother objected to, because she found the language so offensive. They are the pages that describe brutal sexual violence done to a nearly illiterate black womanchild, who then proceeds to write down what has happened to her in her own language, from her own point of view. She does not find rape thrilling; she thinks the rapist looks like a frog with a snake between his legs. How could this not be upsetting? shocking? How could anyone want to hear this? She spoke of "pussy," "titties," the man's "thang." I remember actually trying to censor this passage in Celie's voice as I wrote it. Even I found it almost impossible to let her say what had happened to her as *she* perceived it, without euphemizing it a little. And why? Because once you strip away the lie that rape is pleasant, that rapists have anything at all attractive about them, that children are not permanently damaged by sexual pain, that violence done to them is washed away by fear, silence, and time, you are left with the positive horror of the lives of thousands of children (and who knows how many adults)—lives we are beginning to hear about now even in *People, Newsweek,* and *Time*—who have been sexually abused and who have never been permitted their own language to tell about it.

Celie's stepfather, the rapist, warns her not to tell anybody but God about having been raped. But Celie's community had already made sure she would not feel free even to use the words she knew. In her backward, turn-of-the-century community, the words "penis" and "vagina" did not exist. Indeed, so off limits was any thought of the penis that the closest anyone got to it in language was to call it "the man's thing." As for "vagina"—well, this is how my grandmother taught her girls to bathe:

"Wash down as far as possible, then wash up as far as possible, then wash possible."

Of course if I had written of Celie's rape from the point of view of the rapist or that of the voyeur, very few people—other than feminists—would have been offended. We have been brainwashed to identify with the person who receives pleasure, no matter how perverted; we are used to seeing rape from the rapist's point of view. I could have written that Celie enjoyed her abuse and done it in such pretty, distancing language that many readers would have accepted it as normal. But to do this would have been to betray Celie; not only her experience of rape, but the integrity of her life, her life itself. For it is language more than anything else that reveals and validates one's existence, and if the language we actually speak is denied us, then it is inevitable that the form we are permitted to assume historically will be one of caricature, reflecting someone else's literary or social fantasy.

This is one reason I use the word "mammy" in the book, as a word used by turn-of-the-century black people, instead of "mother," though already in a somewhat pejorative way. It is my hunch that "mammy"—which in the United States conjures up only an immensely fat and black wide-eyed slave of thin Vivien Leigh– or Bette Davis–like white people—is in fact an African word. * For certain it was a word used by early-twentieth-century African-Americans, until it was expropriated and popularized by whites and used to designate a kind of contented, white-folks-comforting black woman of enormous girth, of whom black people felt ashamed. I feel immensely grateful that what little understanding I have of the probable transformation of this word comes from having had a grandfather who, while I was growing up, still used it. This is what he called his mother and this is what he called his children's mother—and as a child, watching the "mammies" in films like *Gone With the Wind,* I wondered why. I knew his mother had been largely Cherokee Indian and was remembered mainly for her meanness and long hair. His wife, my mother's mother, was an obviously oppressed, long-suffering black, black woman, who gave birth to twelve children and who, from pictures and memories that I have of her, apparently never smiled.

There is no reason to try to bring "mammy" back. Its intention in racist books and films was to undermine the integrity of the mother of the black race, and in the minds of many, many people this was accomplished. From this attack on the

* "Ancient Ghanaians were said to have referred to the moon, a maternal symbol, as *mame*, and to the sun, a paternal symbol, as *pape*. Children of the moon, who were the stars, were said to have been called *pickens*. When some of the Ghanaians were brought to the New World as slaves their masters wouldn't let them keep old traditions. But the terms didn't change much. They began calling the father of a slave child pappy, and the mother mammy. The pickens, of course, became pickaninnies."—Carroll Simms, artist, telling a story told to him by another artist, John Biggers, after his return from Ghana in the 1960s. In *Black Art in Houston: The Texas Southern University Experience,* edited by John Edward Weems, introduced by Donald Weisman (College Station: Texas A & M Press, 1978).

black mother figure many of us are still suffering. This is the meaning of the feeling of embarrassment and discomfort we feel even today in the presence of old white Southern-based "classic" racist films. This is the reason many black people cannot even say the word aloud without cringing. It will be a great and amusing day in our nation's future when a film—perhaps many films—will be made about the old plantation South and the story will unfold from a real "mammy's" point of view. Then we will see why the real woman was locked inside the stereotype. It will be like watching a prison break.

For instance, in Norman Yetman's *Life Under the Peculiar Institution** he quotes Fannie Moore, an ex-slave from North Carolina, who recalled her mother quilting: "My mammy she work in the field all day and piece and quilt all night. Then she has to spin enough thread to make four cuts for the white folks every night. Why sometime I never go to bed. Have to hold the light for her to see by. She have to piece quilts for the white folks too."

There they are, "mammy" and daughter, both dead tired, working together through the night. "Why sometime I never go to bed," the daughter says. "Have to hold the light for her to see by."

And that, today, is also what preserving the elders' language is (and it is truly astonishing how much of their language is present tense, which seems almost a message to us to remember that the lives they lived are always current, not simply historical), for it can be a light, held close to them and their times, that illuminates them clearly. A light that helps us really begin to see them, and to comprehend the violence their images and

* *Selections from the Slave Narrative Collections* (New York: Holt, Rinehart and Winston, 1970).

beings have sustained. As in, for example, Al Jolson's famous anti-mammy, anti-black mother, song.

Here is Jolson, a white man. He is on stage before thousands of people, and, since television, before millions. He has blackened his face with burnt cork; he wears a black wig of coarse corkscrew curls. Out of his thin, made up to look fat, white-lipped mouth, as he bends theatrically on one knee, comes . . .

But you remember.

When he sings, there is a kind of jazzy chorus and the backup singers strut and yell. We understand that Jolson is not serious, that his "Mammy" is a joke, and a trivial one. It is as if he's murdered our true grandmothers (Fannie Moore's mammy) before our very eyes.

And yet, because we love the people's voices, and understand why they spoke the way they did, we can see and hear a different mammy, no matter what Al Jolson presents. We can see and hear Fannie Moore's mammy (I imagine her thin, brown, rarely smiling, her eyes red from lack of sleep and sewing all night in poor light). We can see and hear Frederick Douglass's mammy. We can see and hear the longing when she is sold down the river, or Fannie is or Frederick is. We can see and hear the loneliness and the daydreams.

Africa must have seemed a million miles away to the black children who were kidnapped and brought here, as distant as the moon. But even so, many of them tried to walk back, right into the sea. And in America they regularly risked their lives to walk back to, or to find, the woman who brought them into the world and loved them, to whom their return was the essence of "holding up the light for her to see by," through the long dark nights of slavery. Just as to them, the light was her smile. And because the light was held up for the "mammy," light also covered the child. For when we hold up a light in order to see anything outside ourselves more clearly, we illuminate ourselves.

Change Al Jolson into Fannie Moore, or any black enslaved person, and see what happens to his song.

But as of now "mammy" is a used, abused, disposed-of word; and the person to whom it applies has met the same fate. This was emphasized for me when a colleague was telling me about the horrors of the recent Republican convention, one of which was the presence of black entertainers who sang.

Who were these entertainers, I asked. "The Mammies and the Pappies," she replied. She then elaborated on the personalities Reagan's staff had chosen to represent black people at the convention. Her harshest words were reserved for the mammy figure, whom she imagined consoling Ronald Reagan with johnnycake and clabbered milk in the "classic" mammy tradition. "Now don't you worry none, honey," this modern mammy would say, her sequined gown now replacing her apron of old, "them bombs you settin' up in Europe ain't botherin' nobody. And them shiftless shines you cuttin' off of welfare ought to find them some good white folks to work for like I done."

And yet, we can learn from what has happened to "mammy," too. That it is not by suppressing our own language that we counter other people's racist stereotypes of us, but by having the conviction that if we present the words in the context that is or was natural to them, we do not perpetuate those stereotypes, but, rather, expose them. And, more important, we help the ancestors in ourselves and others continue to exist. If we kill off the *sound* of our ancestors, the major portion of us, all that is past, that is history, that is human being is lost, and we become historically and spiritually thin, a mere shadow of who we were, on the earth.

How fortunate, then, that many of us love memories. That

we understand we are who we are largely because of who we have been. And who we have been has come down to us as the vibration of souls we can know only through the sound and structure, the idiosyncrasies of speech. This is especially true for black folk who had no access (especially as slaves) to the visual documentation of painting and later of photography.

Actually I am wrong to think, as I sometimes do, that this love of memories is peculiar to any race or clan. I believe it is a human trait—and for all I know, even a nonhuman animal one—and that what the black, the Native American, and the poor white share in America is common humanity's love of remembering who we are. It is because the language of our memories is suppressed that we tend to see our struggle to retain and respect our memories as unique. And of course our language is suppressed because it reveals our cultures, cultures at variance with what the dominant white, well-to-do culture perceives itself to be. To permit our language to be heard, and especially the words and speech of our old ones, is to expose the depth of the conflict between us and our oppressors and the centuries it has not at all silently raged. It is to realize that behind the back of the man who insisted on being called "master," the "slaves" called him "redneck," "devil," and "peckerwood." It is to learn that every time the real Tonto said "How" aloud to the same racist Wasichu, under his breath he added "stupid," "childish," "asinine," or "unintelligent."

When I finished writing *The Color Purple* I sent it first to a leading black women's magazine, believing they would recognize its value better than anyone. The magazine declined to run an excerpt from it, however, because, according to an editor, "Black people don't talk like that." And I suppose in her mind they never did, and if they did, who cared? Yet Celie speaks in the voice and uses the language of my step-grandmother, Rachel,

LIVING BY THE WORD

an old black woman I loved. Did she not exist; or, in my memories of her, must I give her the proper English of, say, Nancy Reagan?

And I say, yes, she did exist, and I can prove it to you, using the only thing that she, a poor woman, left me to remember her by—the sound of her voice. Her unique pattern of speech. Celie is created out of language. In *The Color Purple* you see Celie because you "see" her voice. To suppress her voice is to complete the murder of her. And this, to my mind, is an attack upon the ancestors, which is, in fact, war against ourselves.

For Celie's speech pattern and Celie's words reveal not only an intelligence that transforms illiterate speech into something that is, at times, very beautiful, as well as effective in conveying her sense of her world, but also what has been done to her by a racist and sexist system, and her intelligent blossoming as a human being despite her oppression demonstrate why her oppressors persist even today in trying to keep her down. For if and when Celie rises to her rightful, earned place in society across the planet, the world will be a different place, I can tell you.

How can you justify enslaving such a person as Celie? segregating or sexually abusing such a person? Her language— all that we have left of her—reveals her as irreducibly human. The answer is you cannot.

She has not accepted an alien description of who she is; neither has she accepted completely an alien tongue to tell us about it. Her being is affirmed by the language in which she is revealed, and like everything about her it is characteristic, hard-won, and authentic.

Bob Marley sings many songs in the black folk English of the Jamaican people. One of my favorites is among the last that he wrote; his mother sang it at his funeral. It is called "Coming

64

In from the Cold." In it he sings, "Don't you let the system make you kill your brotherman," and I can apply this to all of us who are writers and readers. Mrs. Green is mistaken in her belief that the "exposure" of turn-of-the-century Southern black folk language degrades black people, for the language is an intrinsic part of who we are and what has, for good or evil, happened to us. And, amazingly, it has sustained us more securely than the arms of angels. Nowhere is this clearer than in our seemingly illiterate, generally nongrammatical songs, songs that even our enemies admit give us the energy century after century to struggle on through. Mrs. Green apparently doesn't understand yet that when you love people their warts take on a strange beauty of their own. She would be amazed by African and African-American folk painting and sculpture, in which the prettiest, most symmetrical, and correct subject is *never* the one presented. In short, I think what probably most upsets Mrs. Green—who also thought sex should be only heterosexual, and not pleasurable or God-inspired—is the discovery that there is definitely a world view different from her own.

Another line in Marley's song is "Why do you look so sad and so forsaken? Don't you know when one door is closed, many more is opened?" Every time I hear these words I see the old ones who spoke in ways that today means their exclusion from serious conscious life. I see the Jewish woman talking Yiddish, using her tongue but, especially, her hands. I hear the Italian-American putting an "a" on the ends of his words. I see so many of our old ones, like Mammy and Tonto, locked away from us and from reality, imprisoned in the easy stereotype of caricature so that even the real language they spoke by this time appears comical, odd, and more and more foreign and "degrading" to their descendants.

But though the system tries to make us kill our brother/sister humans, by distorting their present and obliterating and ridiculing their past, we are, all of us, those doors of which Marley sings. (And think of all the old ones, including the buffalo soldiers and even Natty Dread himself, Marley brought back in!) The system closed the door on people who sounded like Celie long before I was born. All of us who can *hear* her today open wide the shut doors in ourselves, and in our society.

And when Celie comes through those doors, buffalo soldiers on one side, Shug and Natty Dread and a clutch of dreadlocked Rastas perhaps on the other, and only when Celie comes through those doors; when Celie comes in from the cold of repression, self-hatred, and denial, and only when Celie comes in from the cold—do I come in. And many of you as well. And when all of us and all of the old ones are hugged up inside this enormous warm room of a world we must build very quickly, really, or die of a too shallow mutual self-respect, you will see, with me, through the happy spirits of our grandchildren, such joy as the planet has never seen. And until that day, let us grow to understand a paraphrase of another of our brother Marley's songs. Let us understand that to keep alive in us the speech and the voices of the ancestors is not only to "lively up" the old spirits through the great gift of memory, but to "lively up" our own selves, as well.

And I can personally deliver the message that the old spirits are more alive today than anyone thought.

When I was a little girl, there was a song that was very popular on the gospel station of the radio. It was called: "Will the Circle Be Unbroken?" It is about how death breaks the circle of loved ones on earth, but how, in heaven, "in the sky, Lord, in the sky," this will not be the case. In heaven neither father nor mother will die. Nor little sister, brother, lover, or husband or wife, either. Heaven, according to the song, is different from here.

It is a mournful song, which was written specifically, I

think, about the loss of the songwriter's mother, and it used to make me sad and fearful of losing my own. Over the years I have worried about losing not only my mother and other members of my family, but also poets, singers, philosophers, prophets, political activists. And many of these we have all lost, sometimes to sickness, accident, or disease, sometimes to assassination. But I have found that where there is spiritual union with other people, the love one feels for them keeps the circle unbroken and the bond between us and them strong, whether they are dead or alive. Perhaps that is one of the manifestations of heaven on earth.

After I had finished *The Color Purple* and it was winning prizes and being attacked, I had several extraordinary dream-visits from people I knew before they died and from people who died before I was born, but whose names and sometimes partial histories I knew. This seemed logical and right. But then, at my most troubled, I started to dream of people I'd never heard of and never knew anything about, except, perhaps, in a general way. These people sometimes brought advice, always excellent and upbeat, sometimes just a hug. Once, a dark, heavyset woman who worked in the fields and had somehow lost the two middle fingers of her right hand took hold of my hand lovingly, called me "daughter," and commented supportively on my work. She was only one of a long line of ancestors who came to visit and take my hand that night, all apparently slaves, field workers, and domestics, who seemed to care about and want to reassure me. I remembered her distinctly next morning because I could still feel her plump hand with its missing fingers gently but firmly holding my own.

Since I am not white and not a man and not really Western and not a psychiatrist, I get to keep these dreams for what they mean to me, and I can tell you that I wake up smiling, or crying happily, as the case may be. It seems very simple: Because they know I love them and understand their language, the old ones speak to me. It feels too good to be true!

I wrote this poem the morning after my dream, which I feel was not so much my dream as ours, and which I feel would sustain me forever, though Mrs. Green were joined by millions and my book banned from the planet itself.

> The old ones
> visit me
> in dreams
> to thank me for
> *The Color Purple;*
>
> They tell me,
> Daughter, it's
> the best
> you've ever done.
>
> I can't tell you
> how many rough
> old hands
> I've shook.

Since this dream I have come to believe that only if I am banned from the presence of the ancestors will I know true grief.

1984

. . . .

OPPRESSED HAIR PUTS A CEILING

ON THE BRAIN

[This was a talk I gave on Founders' Day, April 11, 1987, at Spelman College in Atlanta.]

. . .

As some of you no doubt know, I myself was a student here once, many moons ago. I used to sit in these very seats (sometimes still in pajamas, underneath my coat) and gaze up at the light streaming through these very windows. I listened to dozens of encouraging speakers and sang, and listened to, wonderful music. I believe I sensed I would one day return, to be on this side of the podium. I think that, all those years ago, when I was a student here and still in my teens, I was thinking about what I would say to you now.

It may surprise you that I do not intend (until the question-and-answer period perhaps) to speak of war and peace, the economy, racism or sexism, or the triumphs and tribulations of black people or of women. Or even about movies. Though the discerning ear may hear my concern for some of these things in what I am about to say, I am going to talk about an issue even closer to home. I am going to talk to you about hair. Don't give a thought to the state of yours at the moment. Don't be at all alarmed. This is not an appraisal. I simply want to share with you some of my own experiences with our friend hair, and at the most hope to entertain and amuse you.

For a long time, from babyhood through young adulthood mainly, we grow, physically and spiritually (including the intellectual with the spiritual), without being deeply aware of it. In fact, some periods of our growth are so confusing that we don't even recognize that growth is what is happening. We may feel hostile or angry or weepy and hysterical, or we may feel depressed. It would never occur to us, unless we stumbled on a book or person who explained it to us, that we were in fact in the process of change, of actually becoming larger, spiritually, than we were before. Whenever we grow, we tend to feel it, as a young seed must feel the weight and inertia of the earth as it seeks to break out of its shell on its way to becoming a plant. Often the feeling is anything but pleasant. But what is most unpleasant is the not knowing what is happening. I remember the waves of anxiety that used to engulf me at different periods in my life, always manifesting itself in physical disorders (sleeplessness, for instance) and how frightened I was because I did not understand how this was possible.

With age and experience, you will be happy to know, growth becomes a conscious, recognized process. Still somewhat frightening, but at least understood for what it is. Those long periods when something inside ourselves seems to be waiting, holding its breath, unsure about what the next step should be, eventually become the periods we wait for, for it is in those periods that we realize we are being prepared for the next phase of our life and that, in all probability, a new level of the personality is about to be revealed.

A few years ago I experienced one such long period of restlessness disguised as stillness. That is to say, I pretty much withdrew from the larger world in favor of the peace of my personal, smaller one. I unplugged myself from television and newspapers (a great relief!), from the more disturbing members of my extended family, and from most of my friends. I seemed to have reached a ceiling in my brain. And under this ceiling my mind was very restless, although all else about me was calm.

As one does in these periods of introspection, I counted the beads of my progress in this world. In my relationship to my family and the ancestors, I felt I had behaved respectfully (not all of them would agree, no doubt); in my work I felt I had done, to the best of my ability, all that was required of me; in my relationship to the persons with whom I daily shared my life I had acted with all the love I could possibly locate within myself. I was also at least beginning to acknowledge my huge responsibility to the Earth and my adoration of the Universe. What else, then, was required? Why was it that, when I meditated and sought the escape hatch at the top of my brain, which, at an earlier stage of growth, I had been fortunate enough to find, I now encountered a ceiling, as if the route to merge with the infinite I had become used to was plastered over?

One day, after I had asked this question earnestly for half a year, it occurred to me that in my physical self there remained one last barrier to my spiritual liberation, at least in the present phase: my hair.

Not my friend hair itself, for I quickly understood that it was innocent. It was the way I related to it that was the problem. I was always thinking about it. So much so that if my spirit had been a balloon eager to soar away and merge with the infinite, my hair would be the rock that anchored it to Earth. I realized that there was no hope of continuing my spiritual development, no hope of future growth of my soul, no hope of really being able to stare at the Universe and forget myself entirely in the staring (one of the purest joys!) if I still remained chained to thoughts about my hair. I suddenly understood why nuns and monks shaved their heads!

I looked at myself in the mirror and I laughed with happiness! I had broken through the seed skin, and was on my way upward through the earth.

Now I began to experiment: For several months I wore long braids (a fashion among black women at the time) made from the hair of Korean women. I loved this. It fulfilled my fantasy of having very long hair and it gave my short, mildly processed (oppressed) hair a chance to grow out. The young woman who braided my hair was someone I grew to love—a struggling young mother, she and her daughter would arrive at my house at seven in the evening and we would talk, listen to music, and eat pizza or burritos while she worked, until one or two o'clock in the morning. I loved the craft involved in the designs she created for my head. (Basket making! a friend once cried on feeling the intricate weaving atop my head.) I loved sitting between her knees the way I used to sit between my mother's and sister's knees while they braided my hair when I was a child. I loved the fact that my own hair grew out and grew healthy under the "extensions," as the lengths of hair were called. I loved paying a young sister for work that was truly original and very much a part of the black hair-styling tradition. I loved the fact that I did not have to deal with my hair except once every two or three months (for the first time in my life I could wash it every day if I wanted to and not have to do anything further). Still, eventually the braids would have to be taken down (a four-to-seven-hour job) and redone (another seven to eight hours); nor did I ever quite forget the Korean women, who, according to my young hairdresser, grew their hair expressly to be sold. Naturally this information caused me to wonder (and, yes, worry) about all other areas of their lives.

When my hair was four inches long, I dispensed with the hair of my Korean sisters and braided my own. It was only then that I became reacquainted with its natural character. I found it to be springy, soft, almost sensually responsive to moisture. As the little braids spun off in all directions but the ones I tried to encourage them to go, I discovered my hair's willfulness, so like my own! I saw that my friend hair, given its own life, had a sense of humor. I discovered I liked it.

Again I stood in front of the mirror and looked at myself and laughed. My hair was one of those odd, amazing, unbelievable, stop-you-in-your-tracks creations—not unlike a zebra's stripes, an armadillo's ears, or the feet of the electric-blue-footed boobie—that the Universe makes for no reason other than to express its own limitless imagination. I realized I had never been given the opportunity to appreciate hair for its true self. That it did, in fact, have one. I remembered years of enduring hairdressers—from my mother onward—doing missionary work on my hair. They dominated, suppressed, controlled. Now, more or less free, it stood this way and that. I would call up my friends around the country to report on its antics. It never thought of lying down. Flatness, the missionary position, did not interest it. It grew. Being short, cropped off near the root, another missionary "solution," did not interest it either. It sought more and more space, more light, more of itself. It loved to be washed; but that was it.

Eventually I knew *precisely* what hair wanted: it wanted to grow, to be itself, to attract lint, if that was its destiny, but to be left alone by anyone, including me, who did not love it as it was. What do you think happened? (Other than that I was now able, as an added bonus, to comprehend Bob Marley as the mystic his music always indicated he was.) The ceiling at the top of my brain lifted; once again my mind (and spirit) could get outside myself. I would not be stuck in restless stillness, but would continue to grow. The plant was above the ground!

This was the gift of my growth during my fortieth year. This and the realization that as long as there is joy in creation there will always be new creations to discover, or to rediscover, and that a prime place to look is within and about the self. That even death, being part of life, must offer at least one moment of delight.

1987

DEAR JOANNA

[Sometime during the early seventies I was asked to write a letter to an imaginary young black woman, giving her some sense of my own experiences and telling her things she might need to know. I wrote a long letter, which I sent off to the person who asked for it (I no longer recall who this was), but then discovered I wanted to say even more.]

· · ·

Dear Joanna:

Forgive me for writing again so soon. I realize you are busy reading the words of all your other sisters who also love you, but you have been constantly on my mind and each day I think of new things to share with you. Today I wanted to tell you about beauty.

In you, there is beauty like a rock.

So distilled, so unshatterable, so ageless, it will attract great numbers of people who will attempt, almost as an exercise of will (and of no more importance to them than an exercise), to break it. They will try ignoring you, flattering you, joining you, buying you, simply to afford themselves the opportunity of finding the one crack in your stone of beauty by which they may enter with their tools of destruction. Often you will be astonished that, while they pursue their single-minded effort to do this, they do not seem to see your sorrowing face (sorrowing because some of them will have come to you in the disguise of friends, even sisters) or note the quavering of your voice, or the tears of vulnerability in your eyes. To such people, your color, your sex, your*self* make you an object. But an object, strangely, perversely, with a soul. A soul.

It is your soul they want.

They will want to crack it out of the rock and wear it somewhere—not inside them, where it might do them good, but *about* them—like, for example, a feather through their hair, or a scalp dangling from their belt.

As frightening as this is, it has always been so.

Your mother and father, your grandparents, *their* parents, all have had your same beauty like a rock, and all have been pursued, often hunted down like animals, because of it. Perhaps some grew tired of resisting, and in weariness relinquished the stone that was their life. But most resisted to the end. The end, for them, being merely you. Your life. Which is not an end.

That resistance also is your legacy.

Inner beauty, an irrepressible music, certainly courage to say No or Yes, dedication to one's own Gods, affection for one's own spirit(s), a simplicity of approach to life, will survive all of us, through your will.

You are, perhaps, the last unconquered resident on this earth. And must live, in any case, as if it *must* be so.

1973

IN THE CLOSET OF THE SOUL

[At a reading of my work at the University of California at Davis in 1986 I met an African-American couple, both of whom had African names. The wife asked for a copy of a poem to Winnie Mandela I had read, which I gave her. She then asked about my reaction to criticism of the character Mister in *The Color Purple*. She was very intense, beautiful, and genuine, and I wanted to give her an answer worthy of her inquiry. I wrote this essay, which I sent to her.]

Dear Mpinga,

You asked if I was shocked at the hostile reaction of some people, especially some black men, to the character of Mister in the book and more particularly in the movie *The Color Purple*. I believe I replied only half jokingly that no, I was beyond shock. I was saddened by the response, disappointed certainly, but I have felt better as I've tried to put myself in the place of the men (and some women) and tried to understand the source of what appears to be in many a genuine confusion, yes (as you say), but also a genuine pain.

An early disappointment to me in some black men's response to my work—to *The Third Life of Grange Copeland* and *Meridian*, for instance—is their apparent inability to empathize with black women's suffering under sexism, their refusal even to acknowledge our struggles; indeed, there are many black men who appear unaware that sexism exists (or do not even know what it is), or that women are oppressed in virtually all cultures, and if they do recognize there is abuse, their tendency is to minimize it or to deflect attention from it to themselves. This is what happened, to a large extent, with the movie. A book and movie that urged us to look at the oppression of women and children by men (and, to a lesser degree, by women) became the opportunity by which many black men drew attention to themselves—not in an effort to rid themselves of the desire or tendency to oppress women and children, but, instead, to claim that inasmuch as a "negative" picture of them was presented to the world, they were, in fact, the ones *being* oppressed. The people responsible for the picture became, ironically, "outside agitators." We should just go back to the sickness we came from.

It has been black men (as well as black women and Native Americans) who have provided in this culture the most inspiring directions for everyone's freedom. As a daughter of these men I did not hear a double standard when they urged each person to struggle to be free, even if they intended to impart one. When Malcolm said, Freedom, by any means necessary, I thought I knew what he meant. When Martin said, Agitate nonviolently against unjust oppression, I assumed he also meant in the home, if that's where the oppression was. When Frederick Douglass talked about not expecting crops without first plowing up the ground, I felt he'd noticed the weeds in most of our backyards. It is nearly *crushing* to realize there was an assumption on *anyone's* part that black women would not fight injustice except when the foe was white.

I was saddened that, in their need to protect their egos from already well-known-to-be-hostile-and-indifferent white racists (who have made plain for centuries that how they treat us has little to do with the "positive" or "negative" image we present), many black men missed an opportunity to study the character of Mister, a character that I deeply love—not, obviously, for his meanness, oppression of women, and general early boorishness, but because he went deeply enough into himself to find the courage to change. To grow.

It is a mistake to assume that Celie's "meekness" makes her a saint and Mister's brutality makes him a devil. The point is, neither of these people is healthy. They are, in fact, dreadfully ill, and they manifest their dis-ease according to their culturally derived sex roles and the bad experiences early impressed on their personalities. They proceed to grow, to change, to become whole, i.e., well, by becoming more like each other, but stopping short of taking on each other's illness. Celie becomes more self-interested and aggressive; Albert becomes more thoughtful and considerate of others.

At the root of the denial of easily observable and heavily documented sexist brutality in the black community—the assertion that black men don't act like Mister, and if they do, they're justified by the pressure they're under as black men in a white society—is our deep, painful refusal to accept the fact that we are not only the descendants of slaves, but we are also the descendants of slave *owners*. And that just as we have had to struggle to rid ourselves of slavish behavior, we must as ruthlessly eradicate any desire to be mistress or "master." I have not, by any means, read or even seen all the negative reviews of

Mister's character and its implications for blacks in America. However, in the ones I have read, I've been struck by the absence of any analysis of who, in fact, Mister is. Nobody, no critic, that is, has asked this character, "Boy, who your peoples?"

In the novel and in the movie (even more so in the movie, because you can *see* what color people are) it is clear that Mister's father is part white; this is how Mister comes by his run-down plantation house. It belonged to his grandfather, a white man and a slave owner. Mister learns how to treat women and children from his father, Old Mister. Who did Old Mister learn from? Well, from Old *Master*, his slave-owning father, who treated Old Mister's mother and Old Mister (growing up) as slaves, *which they were.* * Old Mister is so riddled with self-hatred, particularly of his black "part," the "slave" part (totally understandable, given his easily imagined suffering during a childhood among blacks and whites who despised each other), that he spends his life repudiating, denigrating, and attempting to dominate anyone blacker than himself, as is, unfortunately, his son. The contempt that Old Mister's father/owner exhibited for his black slave "woman" (Old Mister's mother) is reflected in Old Mister's description of Shug Avery, who, against all odds, Albert loves: "She black as tar, she nappy headed. She got legs like baseball bats." *This is a slave owner's description of a black woman.* But Albert's ability to genuinely love Shug, and find her irresistibly beautiful—black as she is—is a major sign of mother love, the possibility of health; and, since she in her blackness reflects him, an indication that he is at least capable of loving himself. No small feat.

We have been slaves *here* and we have been slaves *there*.

---

* This is not to imply that all sexist cruelty among black people was inherited from white slave owners. On the contrary, in the sections of *The Color Purple* that are set in Africa there is an exploration of the historical oppression of women that is endemic to many traditional African cultures and that continues today.

Our white great-grandfathers abused and sold us *here*, and our black great-grandfathers abused and sold us *there*. This means—should mean—that we are free now. We don't owe them anything but our example of how not to be like them in that way. Slavery forced us to discontinue relating to each other as tribes: we were all in it together. Freedom should force us to stop relating as owner and owned. *If it doesn't, what has it all been for?* What the white racist thinks about us, about anything, is not as important as this question.

But crucial to our development, too, it seems to me, is an acceptance of our actual as opposed to our mythical selves. We are the mestizos of North America. We are black, yes, but we are "white," too, and we are red. To attempt to function as only one, when you are really two or three, leads, I believe, to psychic illness: "white" people have shown us the madness of that. (Imagine the psychic liberation of white people if they understood that probably no one on the planet is genetically "white.") Regardless of who will or will not accept us, including perhaps, our "established" self, we must be completely (to the extent it is possible) who we are. And who we are becomes more obvious to us, I think, as we grow older and more open to the voices of suffering from our own souls.

For instance, I know about Old Mister's father—that he was a slave owner—because he was also my great-great-grandfather. But I didn't begin to *feel* him, *let* myself feel him, until I was in my late thirties. I discovered his very real presence in an odd way: I began to hear him pleading to be let in. I wrote a poem about this called "Family Of"*:

> Sometimes I feel so bad
> I ask myself

* The poems in this essay are from *Horses Make a Landscape Look More Beautiful* by Alice Walker. (San Diego: Harcourt Brace Jovanovich, Inc., 1984.)

Who in the world
Have I murdered?

It is a Wasichu's voice
That asks this question,
Coming from nearly inside of me.

It is asking to be let in, of course.

I am here too! he shouts,
Shaking his fist.
Pay some attention to me!

But if I let him in
What a mess he'll make!
Even now asking who
He's murdered!
Next he'll complain
Because we don't keep a maid!

He is murderous and lazy
And I fear him,
This small, white man;
Who would be neither courteous
Nor clean
Without my help.
By the hour I linger
On his deficiencies
And his unfortunate disposition,
Keeping him sulking
And kicking
At the door.

There is the mind that creates
Without loving, for instance,
The childish greed;
The boatloads and boatloads of tongues . . .

Besides, where would he fit
If I did let him in?
No sitting at round tables
For him!

I could be a liberal
And admit one of his children;
Or be a radical and permit two.
But it is *he* asking
To be let in, alas.

Our mothers learned to receive him occasionally,
Passing as Christ. But this did not help us much.
Or perhaps it made all the difference.

But there. He is bewildered
And tuckered out with the waiting.
He's giving up and going away.
Until the next time.

And murdered quite sufficiently, too, I think,
Until the next time.

I used to read this poem occasionally to my students, but stopped. The young white men present always thought "This small, white man" meant them, and that they were being "murdered" and excluded even in the classroom; the black men and women seemed to think the same thing, and that the "murder" was both literal and justified. They may all have had a point, and the poem does work on that level. However, the impetus for the poem came out of my struggle with my great-great-grandfather, the slave owner and rapist (what *else* was he? I've often racked my brains!) whom I had no intention of admitting into my self. The more I heard him plead, like a damned soul, to be let into my psyche (and it occurred to me that karmic justice being as exact as it is, I might be the only one of his descendants in whom his voice still exists), the more I denounced him as a white man, a killer, destroyer of the planet, a Wasichu, naturally no part of me. Get lost, you old bastard, is essentially what I said. Being a part of me already, however, he couldn't.

I dreamed of him. My image of him at the time—and over a period of years, and still—was of a small, white, *naked*, pale-eyed, pale-haired, oldish white man. Weak-looking: weak, near-sighted eyes, weak limbs. Ineffectual. Hard to imagine him raping anyone—but then, she, my great-great-grandmother, was only eleven.

That is what I learned from relatives when I began to ask questions about "this small, white man," wringing his hands and crying and begging outside my psyche (on his knobby knees) all alone. Already I had found my Indian great-great-grandmother, and she was safely smoking inside my heart.

It took the death of John Lennon to squeeze the old man through. John had been Irish, too (though born in Liverpool). And when he was murdered (and I *loved* him, "white" as he was, for there is no denying the beauty and greatness of his spirit), I felt the price we pay for closing anyone off. To cut anyone out of the psyche is to maim the personality; to suppress any part of the personality is to maim the soul.

And so, I opened the heart of my soul, and there, with the Africans, are the Indian great-great-grandmother and the old white child molester and rapist. Lately I have been urging him to enlarge his personality to include singing or making music on the fiddle. And to stop shouting!

But when I wrote a poem about the peaceful coming together racially, at last, of my psyche, a black male critic wrote the following:

. . . So as I receive Alice Walker's 11th book (she has edited an additional one as well) and her fourth volume of poetry, I face my usual decision: Given my disdain for what she and her work represent, in too large a part, should I assess her work? I know I can count on having to cut through her whimpering, half-balanced neurosis and wonder how on earth to avoid an exercise in negativity. And, of course, all of this contemplation begins before I even open her latest book.

After I open it, the worst slaps at me almost before I can take another breath. Her poem-dedication reads:

> for two who
> slipped away
> almost
> entirely:
> my "part" Cherokee
> great-grandmother
> Tallulah
> (Grandmama Lula)
> on my mother's side
> about whom
> only one
> agreed-upon
> thing
> is known:

her hair was so long
she could sit on it;

and my white (Anglo-Irish?)
great-great-grandfather
on my father's side;
nameless
(Walker, perhaps?),
whose only remembered act
is that he raped
a child:
my great-great-grandmother,
who bore his son,
my great-grandfather,
when she was eleven . . .

So again, here we go with the old Negro refrain of: *me
ain't really a nigger . . . no, no . . . me really a injin*; and
let me point out the rapist in my bloodline to you. The
Negro is the only species who goes around advertising he
or she was raped and has a rapist in his or her bloodline.
It is the kind of twisted pathology that black psychology is
still trying to unravel.

Yet none of this can be taken lightly because Alice Walker
is being pushed by the Liberal mainstream as *the* black
writer in season—while they seek to remove Toni Morri-
son—with her incessant searching for truth and healing in
black life—from that pedestal. But the truth is Mrs. Mor-
rison won't go for the bone of divide-and-conquer that the
Liberals especially like to see black people gnawing at. One
can see their dribble-laden glee when they can find a black
man who through his actions or words attacks a black
woman and vice versa. So, of course, they love Ms. Walker,

lover of queer bourgeois Liberal affectations and deep-down hater of black.

These comments, by black poet and writer K. T. H. Cheat-wood, appeared in a review of my collection of poems *Horses Make a Landscape Look More Beautiful* in the *Richmond* (Virginia) *News Leader*, in the winter of 1984. Unfortunately, in quoting my poem-dedication to my white and Indian ancestors, he left off the most important section:

> Rest in peace.
> The meaning of your lives
> is still
> unfolding.

> Rest in peace.
> In me
> the meaning of your lives
> is still
> unfolding.

> Rest in peace, in me.
> The meaning of your lives
> is still
> unfolding.

> Rest. In me
> the meaning of your lives
> is still
> unfolding.

> Rest. In peace
> in me

the meaning
of our lives
is still
unfolding.

Mr. Cheatwood thinks, apparently, that I should be ashamed to mention, to "advertise" my great-great-grandmother's rape. He assumes an interest, on my part, in being other than black, of being "white." I, on the hand, feel it is my blackness (not my skin color so much as the culture that nurtured me) that causes me to open myself, acknowledge my soul and its varied components, take risks, affirm everyone I can find (for I, too, have been called everything but a child of God), and that inasmuch as my great-great-grandmother was forced to endure rape *and* the birth of a child she couldn't have wanted, as well, the least I *can* do is mention it. In truth, this is all the herstory of her that I know. But if I affirm *that*, then I can at least *imagine* what the rest of her life must have been like. And this, I believe, has some importance for us all.

We are the African and the trader. We are the Indian and the settler. We are the slaver and the enslaved. We are oppressor and oppressed. We are the women and we are the men. We are the children. The ancestors, black and white, who suffered during slavery—and I've come to believe they *all* did; you need only check your own soul to imagine how—grieve, I believe, when a black man oppresses women, and when a black woman or man mistreats a child. They've paid those dues. Surely they bought our gentleness toward each other with their pain.

So, these are my thoughts, Mpinga. I love that, though born in America, you have chosen an African name. I can remember when such an expression of psychic and cultural duality would have been but vaguely understood. But times change, and people do, too. Now such affirmations are almost routine. The infinite faith I have in people's ability to understand anything that makes sense has always been justified, finally, by their behavior. In my work and in myself I reflect black people, women *and* men, as I reflect others. One day even the most self-protective ones will look into the mirror I provide and not be afraid.

Your sister,
Alice

1986

Postscript

In my response to Mpinga I did not touch on what I consider the egregious hyprocrisy of many of the critics of the novel and the movie. In letters sent to the producers of the film while it was being shot (letters threatening picket lines, boycotts, and worse if the script was not submitted to them, prior to filming, for approval), members of the group Blacks Against Black Exploitation of Blacks in the Media made it clear that a primary concern of theirs was not merely the character of Mister but a fear of the "exposure" of lesbianism "in the black community." One of the letters expressed the fear that, just as the use of cocaine skyrocketed in the black community after the showing of *Superfly*, a movie about a racially mixed, black-ghetto hustler, pimp, and dope dealer that many black audiences identified with in the seventies, lesbianism, apparently in their view another "plague," would race through the black community in the eighties. It was also stated that homosexuality was "subject to control" by the community, and that love between black women was okay as long as it wasn't publicly expressed. (This brought to mind the sentiment of white supremacists that they don't mind black people being free, as long as they confine their freedom to some other planet.)

If the concern of critics had sincerely been the depiction of the cruel black male character Mister, as played by Danny Glover (in a film that is, after all, about a black woman, whose struggle is precisely that of overcoming abuse by two particularly unsavory men), they were late in sounding the alarm. What of black actors, men and women, who play CIA agents? U.S. spies? Members of Cointelpro? These characters are used to legitimize real organizations that are involved in assassinating our leaders and heroes around the world and destabilizing and destroying whole Third World *countries* besides. Yet, because they're middle-class, speak standard English, are never permitted to sleep with anybody at all, they are considered decent models for us to have.

In my opinion, it is not the depiction of the brutal behavior of a black male character that is the problem for the critics; after all, many of us have sat in packed theaters where black men have cheered (much as white racists have cheered at images depicting blacks being abused) when a black woman was being terrorized or beaten, or, as in one of Prince's films, thrown in a garbage dumpster. Rather, it is the behavior of the women characters that is objectionable; because whatever else is happening in the novel and the film (and as is true more and more in real life), women have their own agenda, and it does not include knuckling under to abusive men. Women loving women, and expressing it "publicly," if they so choose, is part and parcel of what freedom for women means, just as this is what it means for anyone else. If you are not free to express your love, you are a slave; and anyone who would demand that you enslave yourself by not freely expressing your love is a person with a slaveholder's mentality.

Rather than be glad that the ability to love has not been destroyed altogether in us, some critics complain about the "rightness" of its direction, hiding behind such shockingly trans-

LIVING BY THE WORD

parent defenses as "but what will white people think of us?" Since "white people" are to a large extent responsible for so much of our worst behavior, which is really their behavior copied slavishly, it is an insult to black people's experience in America to make a pretense of caring what they think.

Much of the criticism leveled against me and my work by black men (and some women) has been delivered in arrogance ("I haven't read the book or seen the movie, but. . . ."), ignorance ("I don't think any black people back then had wallpaper. . . ."), bad faith ("I think the author just doesn't like black men; after all, she was married to a white one. . . ."), and without love.* In the end, this simple injustice will be an undeserved burden and worrisome puzzle to our children, our next generation of rebels and poets (Dare they create from the heart? think with their own brain? make decisions that in a treacherous world inevitably involve risk or invite attack?), many of whom write to me frequently about both the film and the book and exhibit a generosity of heart and a tolerance of spirit sadly lacking in some of their parents.

1987

* One shining example of criticism by a black man offered *with* love is the review of *The Color Purple*, the movie, by Carl Dix that appeared in the *Revolutionary Worker*. He expressed concern over the way so many of Celie's problems seemed to be solved by her receiving a house and business left to her by her father (who had been lynched when she was a child). He correctly argues that the inheritance of private property is not a viable solution in terms of the masses of poor people and wishes that this aspect of Celie's existence could have been more progressive. I understand this criticism and feel it does indeed project our thoughts forward into the realm of better solutions for the landless, jobless, and propertyless masses. However, I also feel that for Celie's time—the post-Reconstruction era in the South, whose hallmark was the dispossession of blacks—this solution was in fact progressive; it spoke eloquently of the foresight of her father in his attempt to provide for her in a society where black people's attempts to provide for their coming generations were brutally repressed.

JOURNAL

August 19, 1983

At the hardware store in town I bought snapdragon-yellow paint for the privy. The walls will be yellow, to capture the sun and cheerfulness, and the seat will be marine blue. The door will be oriental red. I realize this sounds like a British telephone booth or perhaps a mailbox—except for the yellow.

Now I shall make a soup for lunch and perhaps put the finishing touches on my speech—or begin on the privy.

But meditate, I must!

Meditation was wonderful—forty-five minutes.

August 20, 1983

And great for peaceful dreams! Last night I had the most extraordinary, beautiful, and exquisite dream about myself and Langston Hughes. We were lovers. And he loved everything about me, even my shoes, which we were looking at, for some reason. We loved walking together. Talking. Laughing. He is so wonderful. We were at Margaret Walker's house when he arrived, but she soon vanished. (It was as if she were the spirit connection.) And for an endless warm time we kissed and hugged and said "I love you. I love you." It was one of the most enjoyable and fulfilling dreams I've ever had. We didn't "make love," we just loved. Deeply. So much so that this morning upon awakening and coming into the big room and facing the rainy day, it all came back to me and I began to cry because it was only a dream. But I felt Langston's presence saying that for us the dream is real. That that can be our space, our place for being together, in love and happy. He asked me if I hadn't found it good and happy and full. And I had to admit I had. He seemed to be, I would guess, in his thirties. Quite handsome and so sweet.

Langston, wherever you are, you make me very happy and I love you.

Perhaps I should do your collected poems, as a publisher has asked me to do. If I did I could be with you more!

October 30, 1983

The U.S. govt. has invaded Grenada. I'm almost too disgusted and angry to write. Maurice Bishop was killed, along with many members of his cabinet. Where are their bodies? I've been wondering. Reagan is a phantom of death. Dispatching Marines, watching them blow up other people, being blown up themselves. Smiling. No one, no soul, lives in the man. This is totally frightening. And I feel the whole country is just waiting for the planet to run aground. Despair, sadness, everywhere.

Meanwhile: Rebecca and I a cozy pair. This morning she was on the sofa in my study and fell asleep on my breast. It was so like the old days(!) when she was a baby. And she is like she was, more like herself. That is: cheerful and loving, affectionate, smart, and funny. The awful New York stranger who confused me with her stepmother seems to be gone. I hope so.

January 7, 1984

No matter in what anger I have written about the black man, I have never once let go of his hand. Though he has kicked me in the shins many times.

And here I am at the end of this notebook, started in 1976, nearly eight years ago!

There have been rough times, but, over all, I feel, continue to feel, blessed. In fact, when I consider the possibilities, and the realities of many other lives, I feel this intensely.

Next month I will be forty. In some ways, I feel my early life's work is done, and done completely. The books that I have produced already carry forward the thoughts that I feel the ancestors were trying to help me pass on. In every generation someone (or two or three) is chosen for this work. Ernest Gaines is one such. Margaret Walker. Langston Hughes and Zora. Toomer. "One plum was left for me. One seed becomes an everlasting singing tree!" Or words to that effect.

Great spirit, I thank you for the length of my days and the fullness of my work. If you wanted me to move on, come home, or whatever is next, I would try to bear it joyfully. Though I am quite joyful here. I love Rebecca and Robert and Casey (Casey makes great fires and loves to be hugged). We are a family. This seemed an impossible dream so often, in this very book. And yet it is real.

Langston was right: the dream *is* real. And if we work at it hard enough, in the dream we will always have a place.

Thank you again. I love you. I love your trees, your sun, your stars and moon and light. Your darkness. Your plums and watermelons and water meadows. And all your creatures and their fur and eyes and feathers and scales.

· · · · · · · · ·

A NAME IS SOMETIMES AN ANCESTOR

SAYING HI, I'M WITH YOU

There are always people in history (or herstory) who help us, and whose "job" it is, in fact, to do this. One way of looking at history (whether oral or written) is as a method that records characteristics and vibrations of our helpers, whose spirits we may feel but of whose objective reality as people who once lived we may not know. Now these people—our "spirit helpers," as indigenous peoples time after time in all cultures have referred to them—always create opportunities that make a meeting with and recognition of them unavoidable.

Sojourner Truth is one such figure for me. Even laying aside such obvious resemblances as the fact that we are both as concerned about the rights of women as the rights of men, and that we share a certain "mystical" bent, Sojourner ("Walker"—in the sense of traveler, journeyer, wanderer) Truth (which "Alice" means in Old Greek) is also my name. How happy I was when I realized this. It is one of those "synchronicities" (some might say conceits) of such reassuring proportions that even when I've been tempted to rename myself "Treeflower" or "Weed" I have resisted.

I get a power from this name that Sojourner Truth and I share. And when I walk into a room of strangers who are hostile to the words of women, I do so with her/our cloak of authority—as black women and beloved expressions of the Universe (i.e., children of God)—warm about me.

She smiles within my smile. That irrepressible great heart rises in my chest. Every experience that roused her passion against injustice in her lifetime shines from my eyes.

This feeling of being loved and supported by the Universe in general and by certain recognizable spirits in particular is bliss. No other state is remotely like it. And perhaps that is what Jesus tried so hard to teach: that the transformation required of us is not simply to be "like" Christ, but to *be* Christ.

The spirit of our helpers incarnates in us, making us more ourselves by extending us far beyond. And to that spirit there is no "beginning" as we know it (although we might finally "know" a historical figure who at one time expressed it) and no end. Always a hello, from the concerned spiritual ancestor you may not even have known you had—but this could strike at any time. Never a good-bye.

1986

· · · · · · · · ·

A THOUSAND WORDS:

A WRITER'S PICTURES OF CHINA

In 1965 I stood next to a fellow American traveler in northern Uganda as he took a picture of a destitute Karamojan tribesman, who was, in fact, dying. The man was a refugee from ancestral lands to the south, now expropriated by another group, and had been forced to eke out what living he could in the barren north. He wore the briefest shredded loincloth, had at most a single tooth, and his eyes were covered with flies. He sat very still for the photograph (he had raised himself at our approach), and as we turned away held out his hand. The photographer gave him a quarter.

No doubt this memory is one reason I never travel with a camera. But another is my belief that human beings are already cameras, and that adding a second camera to the process of seeing (and remembering) shallows, rather than deepens, vision. When the TV commercial declares Kodak "the nation's story-teller," I shudder, because I realize our personal culture is about to become as streamlined as our public. But perhaps only poets and writers feel this.

In June of 1983 I went to China with a group of twelve American women writers that included Paule Marshall (our delegation leader), Nellie Wong, Blanche Boyd, Tillie Olsen, Lisa Alther, and my friend and travel companion Susan Kirschner, who took many beautiful pictures of our trip with a real camera, which she has shared with me, as I wish to share these imaginary or mental "snaps" with her and with the other members of our group.

1

This is a picture of Susan and me at the San Francisco airport en route to China! We are leaning against the ticket counter furiously scribbling notes to our loved ones. I have chosen the same card for my daughter as for my companion. On a white background in large black letters above a vibrant red heart are the words I AM SO-O-O HAPPY WITH YOU!

So why am I going to China?

Whenever I fly, I fear I will not return to Earth except in shreds. As the plane lifts off I look at the Earth with longing and send waves of love to cover it as I rise.

How could anyone be foolish enough to leave the ground?

But you, I write to both of them, will also understand this contradiction in me: that I must fly to see even more of the Earth I love.

2

In this one Susan and I are on the plane somewhere over the Pacific reading identical copies of *The True Story of Ah Q* by the immortal Lu Hsun and drinking innumerable cups of Japanese green tea. In this story (1921), by the "father" of modern Chinese literature, a penniless peasant blunders his way into revolutionary pretense among local villagers, who hang him for his troubles. Lu Hsun depicts Ah Q as a foolish, childish person with no understanding of his emotions or his fate. We finish reading it about the same time and look at each other in quizzical disbelief. We feel Lu Hsun has condescended to his character, in precisely the way white Southern writers have condescended to their characters who are black. And as male writers condescend to characters who are women. That he, in fact, cannot believe a peasant capable of understanding his own oppression, his own life. Since the story is also exceedingly dull, we wonder what the Chinese value in it, beyond the fact that it is perhaps the first attempt to portray a Chinese peasant in fiction.

3

This one shows our arrival in Beijing. Not the actual landing and meeting with our interpreters and Chinese writer hosts, but the long drive from airport into town. Our first awareness is that though China's people population is phenomenal, its *tree* population is more so: and they are a kind of planned magic. From the air they're hardly visible because of the dust that sweeps down from the northern desert steppes and turns the landscape dun and yellow. And even when they first appear they seem modest and young, and one thinks of them in future tense. How grand they will look at eighty, and so on. But by the time one arrives on the streets of Beijing and notices veritable layers of trees five and six rows deep lining the broad boulevards a wonderful relief comes over the mind.

For one feels irresistibly drawn to people who would plant and care for so many millions of trees—and a part of this traveler relaxed. Because, for one thing, the planting of trees demonstrates a clear intention to have a future and a definite disinterest in war.

4

In this one, five members of our group are standing around the limited but adequate bar (orange crush, mineral water, beer, Coca-Cola) at the end of our floor in a hotel in Beijing. It is the day of our first long outing through the dusty streets of the city. Everyone is hot and thirsty. They are trying to decide whether to have orange crush, mineral water, or beer, like Americans who know what is going on. The look of dismay on their faces is because I have just walked up to the counter and said to the barkeep: I'll have a Coke.

I take the Coke into the room I share with Susan, drink some, and pour some out the window in libation. I save the bottle cap with "Coca-Cola" written in Chinese. Wherever I go in the world I buy one Coca-Cola in memory of the anonymous black woman who is said to have created it (probably on the theory that if you dope your masters—I have heard that Coke used to have coke in it—they're more pleasant).

I never heard of that, says Susan.

And I tell her it is the one thing I remember from my high-school graduation day. Our commencement speaker, Mr. Bullock, a horticulturist of stature from Atlanta, tried for thirty minutes to inspire pride of heritage in us by listing name upon illustrious name of heroic and creative black folk. People nodded. But when he said: Even Coca-Cola was invented by a black woman, everybody snapped awake. For didn't most of us drink this part of the heritage every day?

I tell Susan that in Collonwalde, the Coca-Cola mansion outside Atlanta, there is a statue of a black woman in the foyer, but nobody I asked about her seemed to know who she was or why she's there.

I laugh. It doesn't matter, really (though what a story there must be behind this story, I think). There's too much sugar in

Coke. I'm sure the original was much better. It may even have been created as a medicine. We run that down a little, start talking about the two most insidious poisons loose in the world today: sugar and cocaine; and soon drift off to sleep.

5

In this one I am wearing a large mulberry-colored coat several sizes too big, a long grape-colored scarf, a Chinese peasant hat the size of an umbrella, and am carrying a cane with a dragon carved on it. We have just stopped twenty miles upriver from the town of Guilin (after a stunning boat ride through mountains that look like stone trees), and the peasant merchants from the surrounding countryside have ambushed us on the shore. Their one American word is "hello," which they say with the same off-key intonation that I'm sure we say "nee-how" (phonetic Chinese for "hello"). In their mouths it becomes a totally different word. It is like meeting a long line of people and each one solemnly greets you with "Elbow." I fantasize that my "nee-how" probably sounds like, say, the Chinese word for "foot" to them. So all during this trip I've been smiling and saying "hello" and they've been hearing "foot, foot, foot."

Looking closely at this picture I see that I am also wearing very baggy pants. In fact, everything I'm wearing is several sizes too large. I realize we were asked by our tour leader not to wear tight, uncomfortable, or revealing clothes, but the overall looseness of my attire appears extreme.

I suspect, looking at this picture, in which I look ridiculous, but regal, that this outsize dressing is typical of people—especially women—who grow up in families whose every other member is larger than they are. Which is true in my family. We can't believe we're as small as we are. And so, we dress ourselves as if we were they.

6

This is a picture of a university dormitory in Guilin. It is early evening as Susan and I walk across the campus on our way to visit families of Susan's Chinese acquaintances in Portland. As is true everywhere in China, there is no wasted electricity (lighting is mellow rather than bright; forty watts rather than a hundred) and no unused space. In rooms smaller than those two U.S. college students would share, five and six students bunk. Freshly washed clothes hang everywhere inside the rooms, and outside the windows on long bamboo poles. The students we meet on the path are returning to the classrooms, which double as places of study at night. We watch rows and rows of them bent silently, intently, over their books.

Of course I think of Hampton Institute, Tuskegee, the early days of Morris Brown, Morehouse, and Spelman, black colleges started just after the Civil War in barracks and basements: poor, overcrowded, but determined to educate former peasants and slaves; schools that have also, like the Chinese schools, managed against great odds to do just that.

7

You would never believe, from this photograph, that I am sitting on the Great Wall of China. I look bored. I look unhappy. There is that tense line around my mouth that means I'll never come thousands of miles to see more of man's folly again. What I hate about the Great Wall is the thought of all the workers' bodies buried in it. I hate the vastness and barrenness of its location. I hate the suffering the women and children attached to the builders endured. I hate its—let's face it, I hate walls.

Susan dashes ahead of me looking for the best view. But the wall tires me, instantly. It is the concrete manifestation of so much that is wrong (a kind of primitive MX). What a stupid waste, I am thinking, in the photograph. A lot of flowers never sniffed. A lot of dancing never done.

The brochure about the wall says that the invaders, finding the Great Wall indeed impenetrable, simply got over it by bribing the guards.

The Great Wall is redeemed by only one thing: over each battlement portal (through which hand-propelled missiles must have whistled) there is a tiny decoration, serving no purpose whatsoever except to refresh the eye. And here is where the writer could benefit from having had a camera other than herself, because I feel deeply about this decoration, this modest attempt at art. I send mental salutations to the artist(s). But now I cannot remember what precisely the decoration is: is it a curled line, horizontal and short, like those on the windows of brownstones? Is it the missing flower? Or is it two straight lines from a hexagram symbolizing war, which I have mistaken for peace?

8

This one is of me and Susan walking across T'ien An Men Square looking at the many fathers out for a stroll with their female children. They all look interested, relaxed, happy. Susan stops one little girl and her father and asks if she may take a picture. At first he looks suspicious, or, more accurately, puzzled. We begin to ooh and aah over his child, a serene three-year-old with an enormous red ribbon in her hair. He understands. And beams with pride. Then we notice that street signs at crossings between the Forbidden City and the square depict just such a pair as we photographed: pearl gray against a blue background without letters of any kind, the outline of a father and daughter holding hands, crossing the street.

We are made incomparably happy by this: I think of my daughter and her father. Susan, I know, thinks of her husband, John, at home with their girls. We look at each other with enormous grins. Thinking of fathers and daughters all over the world and wishing them luck.

9

This one shows us sitting down in the middle of the square looking dissatisfied. We look this way because we both really like Beijing. Miraculously feel at peace here. It is true that the dust gives us coughing fits and my eyes feel gritty from the smog, but overall we are pleased with the wide, clean boulevards, the rows of linden trees that sparkle like jewels in every breeze, the calm, meditative motion of thousands of bikers who pedal as if they're contemplating eternity rather than traffic. At night we, like the Chinese, are drawn to the streets. There is no sense of danger. No fear. People look at us, mildly curious. We look back. Occasionally there is a spoken greeting. A smile.

What is it about Beijing that is so seductive? Susan muses. We consider the dimness of the lights at night. The way the few cars and trucks do not use their headlights, only their parking lights. The way homes seem to be lit by candles. How there is very little neon. Nothing that blinks, flashes, or winks. The softness this gives the evening. The night. How strolling through this softness and hearing, through an open window, someone practicing cello or flute is a satisfying experience. And how the mind begins to think religious thoughts but in a new way.

When we first arrived, we thought Beijing a drab and ugly city because of the gray buildings and perpetual dust. Now, after six days, we find it beautiful enough not to want to leave, though neither of us speaks more than three words of Chinese.

In the West, Susan says, the cities are built to impress you with *themselves*. They are all-important. Here, the people are most important, and the buildings are backdrop.

10

Something else occurs to me from this next picture—the one of me wearing both the Chinese ring and the cloisonné bracelet I bought at the Friendship Store. People are more important than what they wear. Everyone wears essentially the same thing: trousers and shirt. And everyone is neat, clean, and adequately dressed. No one wears make-up or jewelry. At first, faces look dull, as a natural tree would look if Christmas trees were the norm. But soon one becomes conscious of the wonderful honesty natural faces convey. An honesty more interesting than any ornament. And a vulnerability that make-up and jewelry would mask.

Except in Shanghai, which resembles a large port city of the West, the Chinese do not have the faces of killers we've become used to in America (where the killer look is encouraged and actually desired); and even the soldiers, very young and wearing straw sandals or black cloth slippers, look gentle and relatively content

11

In all of China there is nothing and no one more beautiful than the writer Ding Ling. She is short and brown and round. She is also "old." But these attributes alone, which connect her to great masses of women throughout the world, do not make her beautiful. It is a puzzle, at first, what does. In this photograph she is listening to Madame Kang Ke Qing tell our group about the Long March and is swinging her foot slightly, as if to keep it awake. Madame has talked for three hours and told us most of the information about the Women's Federation (which she heads) we'd already read (that the Women's Federation "reeducates" those who would practice female infanticide, for instance).

I have drunk so much tea I am afraid to stand up. But Ding Ling? It is not tea she has drunk. She has drunk patience. Imprisoned by reactionaries and radicals, Kuomintang and Communists, presumed dead at least twice, to national mourning, her young common-law husband executed by firing squad two months after the birth of their child, herself locked in solitary confinement for ten months by Mao Zedong's wife, Jiang Qing, imprisoned and separated from her present husband, Chen Ming, for six years, under the Gang of Four, this small brown round "old" woman—who claps her hands like a child when Susan asks if she will be photographed with me—has, through everything (banishment to Manchuria to raise chickens among the peasants, whom she taught, as they taught her), simply continued to write. Powerful story after story, novel after novel, over a period of fifty years. And though beaten bloody by the Red Guards during the Cultural Revolution (for having been, among other things, famous) and forced to parade through the streets wearing a blackened face and a dunce's cap, she holds no bitterness, only saying, of all her travails—illnesses, children lost, books and notes destroyed—mainly, I lost time.

At nearly eighty she says things like: Oh, to be sixty-seven again!

After meeting Ding Ling, who is radiant with life and writing still, it becomes amusing and finally ludicrous to hear one of our American writers complain in city after city, to group after group, that she was unable to write most of her life "because of her children."

12

In this picture I have just been told by an editor of a Shanghai literary magazine that my novel *The Color Purple* is being translated into Chinese. I am delighted. Especially when she looks me warmly in the eye and says, with a beautiful accent, mocking my surprise: But Alice, it is a very *Chinese* story. She tells me further that two of my stories have already appeared in translation and that the woman who translated them (and who will translate the novel) wanted to meet me but was afraid I'd want to talk about copyrights.

I don't. What interests me is how many of the things I've written about women certainly do, in China, look Chinese: the impact of poverty, forced sex and childbearing, domination as a race *and* a caste (before the Chinese Revolution); the struggle to affirm solidarity with women, as women, and the struggle to attain political, social, and economic equality with men.

But I am disturbed that a young Chinese writer of my generation, Yu Loujing, who is writing stories and novels similar in theme to mine in China, is banned. Whenever we ask about her there is a derisive response. She is only "writing out of her own bitter experiences," they say, as if this is a curse. "She is perpetuating bourgeois individualism." One of our hosts even goes so far as to accuse her of libel.

Still, though we do not meet her, and her books (not yet in English translation) can be bought only on the black market, she is the writer in China, next to Ding Ling, who intrigues me. She has written, for instance, about being raped by her husband on their wedding night, and of her hatred of it; an experience shared by countless women around the world (by now we understand there does not *have* to be blood on the sheets). For this bravery alone I feel the women of China will eventually love her. In fact, already do. For though she is scorned by the literary establishment—and by the Chinese Writers Union in particular—all her books are underground best sellers.

13

In this one, one of our hosts is singing "Old Black Joe" under the impression that this will prove she knows something about American blacks. There is deep sadness in this picture, as we realize that the Chinese, because of China's years of isolation, have missed years of black people's struggle in the United States. No Martin, no Malcolm, no Fannie Lou. No us. I want to move closer to Paule Marshall and put my arms around her, and I want her to hug me back. Here we are, two black women (thank the Universe we *are* two!), once again facing a racial ignorance that depresses and appalls. Our singing host was once in America, in the fifties, she says, and was taught this song as part of her English lessons. This is one of the songs U.S.-trained Chinese learned in America and brought back to teach others throughout China.

I explain the reactionary nature of the song. But the energy required to do this nearly puts me to sleep. Nor could I foretell that from this point in the trip everywhere I go I will be asked to sing. To teach the Chinese "a new song." I sing (one of my secret ambitions, actually); the irony of being asked, as a black person, not lost on me for a second. I start out with the Reverend Dorsey ("We Shall Overcome") and end up with Brother Lennon ("Hold On"). But it is really James Weldon Johnson's Negro National Anthem that is required ("Lift Ev'ry Voice and Sing"); and I am embarrassed to say I could not recall all the words. This I consider the major personal failure of the trip.

Lift ev'ry voice and sing
Till earth and heaven ring
Ring with the harmonies of liberty
Let our rejoicing rise
High as the listening skies

Let it resound
Loud as the rolling seas

Sing a song
Full of faith that the dark past has taught us
Sing a song
Full of the hope that the present has brought us
Facing the rising sun of our new day begun
Let us march on till victory is won.

Stony the road we trod
Bitter the chastening rod
Felt in the days when hope unborn had died
Yet with a steady beat
Have not our weary feet
Come to the place, Oh, where our [ancestors] sighed?*

We have come
Over a way that with tears has been watered
We have come
Treading our path through the blood of the slaughtered
Out from the gloomy past till now we stand at last
Where the white gleam of our bright star is cast.

14

In this one, three young men from Africa are talking. They
are from Chad, Uganda, and Somalia, and have been studying
medicine in China for seven years. In a few weeks they will be
going home.

* I have replaced the original "fathers" with "ancestors," believing that Brother Johnson,
a sometime progressive in his day (1871–1938) and an artist, in any event, would
understand that our fathers were not by themselves when they sighed.

They teach us, but that is all, one of them says. There's no such thing as going up to the professor outside the class.

And if the Chinese should invite you to their home, says another, they make sure it's dark and the neighbors don't see. And the girls are told definitely not to go out with us.

But why is this? I ask, heart sinking over the brothers' isolation. But marveling that they all study medicine in Chinese.

Because the Chinese do not like black people, one says. Some are nice, but some call us black devils. They don't like anyone really but themselves. They pretend to like whites because that is now the correct line, and they're all over white Americans because they want American technology.

As we talk, I am reminded of Susan's face one evening after she'd been talking, for over an hour, with our interpreters. She was happy because they had appeared interested in and asked innumerable questions about American blacks. Only after I pointed out that they could have put the same questions directly *to* American blacks (Paule and me) did her mood change.

That's right, she said. Damn it.

The next evening a continuation of the questions about blacks was attempted, but Susan was ready, and annoyed. Any questions about blacks, ask Paule and Alice. Both are black, and Alice is even a peasant! she said. And that night her face was even happier than before.

15

This is a picture of our hotel room in Hong Kong. Susan is standing in the doorway preparing to leave. She is carrying a beautiful cello she bought for her husband in Shanghai (which she laughingly says is my color *and* shape). But is it my tone? I reply.

I have been ill the last couple of days of the trip, and she has been mother, sister, and nurse. All of which adds up to:

Let's get a doctor up here quick! It is mostly exhaustion and I am spending my last morning in Hong Kong in bed. Later I will get up and catch a plane to Hawaii, where my companion is waiting to meet me.

Now that we are out of Mainland China there is an eagerness to be gone entirely. I look down on the bay and at the hills of Hong Kong and all I can think about is San Francisco. China already seems a world away. And is. Only a few images remain: the peasant who makes 10,000 yuan (about $15,000) a year and has built a nice two-story house that fills his eyes with pride; the tired face of Shen Rong, the writer whose long short story "Approaching Middle Age" (about the struggle of Chinese women professionals to "do it all") I watched dramatized on Beijing TV; the faces of people depicted in statues commemorating the Chinese Revolution: strong, determined, irresistible; Ding Ling; and the city of Beijing itself, which of all the marvels I saw is what I like best of the New China.

But the finest part of the trip has been sharing it with Susan. Over the years we have incited each other to travel: Let's go to Mexico! Let's go to Grenada! Let's go to China! And now we have. She stands worriedly at the hotel door, now admiring, now cursing the rather large cello that grows larger by the second, that she's not sure she should have bought. Do you think they'll let it on the plane? she frets. Will it need its own seat? And, are you *positive* you're okay? she asks, striding out the door.

1985

- - - - - - - - -

JOURNEY TO NINE MILES

By five o'clock we were awake, listening to the soothing slapping of the surf, and watching the sky redden over the ocean. By six we were dressed and knocking on my daughter's door. She and her friend Kevin were going with us (Robert and me) to visit Nine Miles, the birthplace of someone we all loved, Bob Marley. It was Christmas Day, bright, sunny, and very warm and the traditional day of thanksgiving for the birth of someone sacred.

I missed Bob Marley when his body was alive, and I have often wondered how that could possibly be. It happened, though, because when he was singing all over the world, I was living in Mississippi, being political, digging into my own his/herstory, writing books, having a baby—and listening to local music, B. B. King, and the Beatles. I liked dreadlocks, but only because I am an Aquarian; I was unwilling to look beyond the sexism of Rastafarianism. The music stayed outside my consciousness.

It didn't help either that the most political and spiritual of reggae music was suppressed in the United States, so that "Stir It Up," and not "Natty Dread" or "Lively Up Yourself" or "Exodus," was what one heard. And then, of course, there *was* disco, a music so blatantly soulless as to be frightening, and impossible to do anything to but exercise.

I first really *heard* Bob Marley when I was in the throes of writing a draft of the screenplay for *The Color Purple*. Each Monday I drove up to my studio in the country, a taxing three-hour drive, worked steadily until Friday, drove back to the city, and tried to be two parents to my daughter on weekends. We kept in touch by phone during the week, and I had the impression that she was late for school every day and living on chocolates. (No *way*! She always smiled innocently.)

My friends Jan and Chris, a white couple nearby, seeing my stress, offered their help, which I accepted in the form of dinner at their house every night after a day's work on the script. One night after yet another sumptuous meal, we pushed back the table and, in our frustration at the pain that rides on the seat next to joy in life (cancer, pollution, invasions, the bomb), began dancing to reggae records: UB-40, Black Uhuru . . . Bob Marley. I was transfixed. It was hard to believe the beauty of the soul I heard in "No Woman No Cry," "Coming In from the Cold," "Could You Be Loved?," "Three Little Birds," and "Redemption Song." Here was a man who loved his roots, even after he'd been nearly assassinated in his own country, and knew they extended to the ends of the earth. Here was a soul who loved Jamaica and loved Jamaicans and loved *being* a Jamaican (nobody got more pleasure out of the history, myths, traditions, and language of Jamaica than Bob Marley) but who knew it was not meant to limit itself, or even could, to an island of any sort. Here was the radical peasant-class, working-class consciousness that fearlessly denounced the Wasichus (the greedy and destructive) and did it with such grace you could dance to it. Here was a man of extraordinary sensitivity, political acumen, spiritual power, and sexual wildness; a free spirit if ever there was one. Here, I felt, was my brother. It was as if there had been a great and gorgeous light on all over the world, and somehow I'd missed it. Every night for the next two months I listened to Bob Marley. I danced with his spirit—so much more alive still than many people walking around. I felt my own dreadlocks begin to grow.

Over time, the draft of the script I was writing was finished. My evenings with my friends came to an end. My love of Marley spread easily over my family, and it was as neophyte rastas, having decided that "rasta" for us meant a commitment to a religion of attentiveness and joy, that we appeared when we visited Jamaica in 1984.

What we saw is a ravaged land, a place where people, often rastas, eat out of garbage cans and where, one afternoon in a beach café during a rainstorm, I overheard a thirteen-year-old boy offer, along with some Jamaican pot, his eleven-year-old sister (whose grownup's earrings looked larger, almost, than her face) to a large, hirsute American white man (who blushingly declined).

The car we rented, from a harried, hostile dealer who didn't even seem to want to tell us where to buy gas, had already had two flats. On the way to Nine Miles it had three more. Eventually, however, after an agonizing seven hours from Negril, where we were staying, blessing the car at every bump in the road, to encourage it to live through the trip, we arrived.

Nine Miles, because it is nine miles from the nearest village of any size, is one of the stillest and most isolated spots on the face of the earth. It is only several houses, spread out around the top of a hill. There are small, poor farms, with bananas appearing to be the predominant crop.

Several men and many children come down the hill to meet our car. They know we've come to visit Bob. They walk with us up the hill where Bob Marley's body is entombed in a small mausoleum with stained-glass windows; the nicest building in Nine Miles. Next to it is a small one-room house where Bob and his wife, Rita, lived briefly during their marriage. I think of how much energy Bob Marley had to generate to project himself into the world beyond this materially impoverished place; and of how exhausted, in so many of his later photographs, he looked. On the other hand, it is easy to understand—listening to the deep stillness that makes a jet soaring overhead sound like the buzzing of a fly—why he wanted to be brought back to his home village, back to Nine Miles, to rest. We see the tomb from a distance of about fifty feet, because we cannot pass through, or climb over, an immense chain-link fence that has recently been erected to keep the too eager (and apparently destructive and kleptomaniacal) tourists at bay. One thing that I like very much: built into the hill facing Bob's tomb is a permanent stage. On his birthday, February 6, someone tells us, people from all over the world come to Nine Miles to sing to him.

The villagers around us are obviously sorry about the fence. Perhaps we were not the ones intended to be kept out? Their faces seem to say as much. They are all men and boys. No women or girls among them. On a front porch below the hill I see some women and girls, studiously avoiding us.

One young man, the caretaker, tells us that, though we can't go in, there *is* a way we can get closer to Bob. I almost tell him I could hardly *be* any closer to Bob and still be alive, but I don't want to try to explain. He points out a path that climbs the side of the hill, and we—assisted by half a dozen of the more agile villagers—take it. It passes through bananas and weeds, flowers, past goats tethered out of the sun, past chickens.

Past the home, one says, of Bob Marley's cousin, a broken but gallant-looking man in his fifties, nearly toothless, and with a gentle and generous smile. He sits in his tiny, bare house and watches us. His face is radiant with the pride of relationship.

From within the compound now we hear singing. Bob's songs come from the lips of the caretaker, who says he and Bob were friends. That he loved Bob. Loved his music. He sings terribly. But perhaps this is only because he is, though about the age Bob would have been now, early forties, lacking his front teeth. He is very dark, and quite handsome, teeth or no. And it is his humble, terrible singing—as he moves proprietarily about the yard where his friend is enshrined—that makes him so. It is as if he sings Bob's songs *for* Bob, in an attempt to animate the tomb. The little children are all about us, nearly underfoot. Beautiful children. One little boy is right beside me. He is about six, of browner skin than the rest—who are nearer to black—with curlier hair. He looks like Bob.

I ask his name. He tells me. I have since forgotten it. As we linger by the fence, our fingers touch. For a while we hold hands. I notice that over the door to the tomb someone has plastered a bumper sticker with the name of Rita Marley's latest album. It reads: "Good Girls Culture." I am offended by it; there are so many possible meanings. For a moment I try to imagine the sticker plastered across Bob's forehead. It drops off immediately, washed away by his sweat (as he sings and dances in the shamanistic trance I so love) and his spirit's inability to be possessed by anyone other than itself, and Jah. The caretaker says Rita erected the fence. I understand the necessity.

Soon it is time to go. We clamber back down the hill to the car. On the way down the little boy who looks like Bob asks for money. Thinking of our hands together and how he is so like Bob must have been at his age, I don't want to give him money. But what else can I give him, I wonder.

I consult "the elders," the little band of adults who've gathered about us.

"The children are asking for money," I say. "What should we do?"

"You should give it" is the prompt reply. So swift and unstudied is the answer, in fact, that suddenly the question seems absurd.

"They ask because they have none. There is nothing here."

"Would Bob approve?" I ask. Then I think, Probably. The man has had himself planted here to fund the village.

"Yes" is the reply. "Because he would understand."

Starting with the children, but by no means stopping there, because the grownups look as expectant as they, we part with some of our "tourist" dollars, realizing that tourism is a dead thing, a thing of the past; that no one can be a tourist anymore, and that, like Bob, all of us can find our deepest rest at home.

It is a long, hot, anxious drive that we have ahead of us. We make our usual supplications to our little tin car and its four shiny tires. But even when we have another flat, bringing us to our fourth for the trip, it hardly touches us. Jamaica is a poor country reduced to selling its living and its dead while much of the world thinks of it as "real estate" and a great place to lie in the sun; but Jamaicans as a people have been seen in all their imperfections and beauty by one of their own and fiercely affirmed, even from the grave, and loved. There is no poverty, only richness in this. We sing "Redemption Song" as we change the tire; feeling very Jamaica, very Bob, very rasta, very *no woman no cry.*

1986

・   ・   ・   ・   ・   ・   ・   ・   ・

MY DAUGHTER SMOKES

My daughter smokes. While she is doing her homework, her feet on the bench in front of her and her calculator clicking out answers to her algebra problems, I am looking at the half-empty package of Camels tossed carelessly close at hand. Camels. I pick them up, take them into the kitchen, where the light is better, and study them—they're filtered, for which I am grateful. My heart feels terrible. I want to weep. In fact, I do weep a little, standing there by the stove holding one of the instruments, so white, so precisely rolled, that could cause my daughter's death. When she smoked Marlboros and Players I hardened myself against feeling so bad; nobody I knew ever smoked these brands.

She doesn't know this, but it was Camels that my father, her grandfather, smoked. But before he smoked "ready-mades"—when he was very young and very poor, with eyes like lanterns—he smoked Prince Albert tobacco in cigarettes he rolled himself.

I remember the bright-red tobacco tin, with a picture of Queen Victoria's consort, Prince Albert, dressed in a black frock coat and carrying a cane.

The tobacco was dark brown, pungent, slightly bitter. I tasted it more than once as a child, and the discarded tins could be used for a number of things: to keep buttons and shoelaces in, to store seeds, and best of all, to hold worms for the rare times my father took us fishing.

By the late forties and early fifties no one rolled his own anymore (and few women smoked) in my hometown, Eatonton, Georgia. The tobacco industry, coupled with Hollywood movies in which both hero and heroine smoked like chimneys, won over completely people like my father, who were hopelessly addicted to cigarettes. He never looked as dapper as Prince Albert, though; he continued to look like a poor, overweight, overworked colored man with too large a family; black, with a very white cigarette stuck in his mouth.

I do not remember when he started to cough. Perhaps it was unnoticeable at first. A little hacking in the morning as he lit his first cigarette upon getting out of bed. By the time I was my daughter's age, his breath was a wheeze, embarrassing to hear; he could not climb stairs without resting every third or fourth step. It was not unusual for him to cough for an hour.

It is hard to believe there was a time when people did not understand that cigarette smoking is an addiction. I wondered aloud once to my sister—who is perennially trying to quit— whether our father realized this. I wondered how she, a smoker since high school, viewed her own habit.

It was our father who gave her her first cigarette, one day when she had taken water to him in the fields.

"I always wondered why he did that," she said, puzzled, and with some bitterness.

"What did he say?" I asked.

"That he didn't want me to go to anyone else for them," she said, "which never really crossed my mind."

So he was aware it was addictive, I thought, though as annoyed as she that he assumed she would be interested.

I began smoking in eleventh grade, also the year I drank numerous bottles of terrible sweet, very cheap wine. My friends and I, all boys for this venture, bought our supplies from a man who ran a segregated bar and liquor store on the outskirts of town. Over the entrance there was a large sign that said COLORED. We were not permitted to drink there, only to buy. I smoked Kools, because my sister did. By then I thought her toxic darkened lips and gums glamorous. However, my body simply would not tolerate smoke. After six months I had a chronic sore throat. I gave up smoking, gladly. Because it was a ritual with my buddies—Murl, Leon, and "Dog" Farley—I continued to drink wine.

My father died from "the poor man's friend," pneumonia, one hard winter when his bronchitis and emphysema had left him low. I doubt he had much lung left at all, after coughing for so many years. He had so little breath that, during his last years, he was always leaning on something. I remember once, at a family reunion, when my daughter was two, that my father picked her up for a minute—long enough for me to photograph them—but the effort was obvious. Near the very end of his life, and largely because he had no more lungs, he quit smoking. He gained a couple of pounds, but by then he was so emaciated no one noticed.

When I travel to Third World countries I see many people like my father and daughter. There are large billboards directed at them both: the tough, "take-charge," or dapper older man, the glamorous, "worldly" young woman, both puffing away. In these poor countries, as in American ghettos and on reservations, money that should be spent for food goes instead to the tobacco companies; over time, people starve themselves of both food and air, effectively weakening and addicting their children, eventually eradicating themselves. I read in the newspaper and in my gardening magazine that cigarette butts are so toxic that if a baby swallows one, it is likely to die, and that the boiled water from a bunch of them makes an effective insecticide.

My daughter would like to quit, she says. We both know the statistics are against her; most people who try to quit smoking do not succeed.*

There is a deep hurt that I feel as a mother. Some days it is a feeling of futility. I remember how carefully I ate when I was pregnant, how patiently I taught my daughter how to cross a street safely. For what, I sometimes wonder; so that she can wheeze through most of her life feeling half her strength, and then die of self-poisoning, as her grandfather did?

But, finally, one must feel empathy for the tobacco plant itself. For thousands of years, it has been venerated by Native Americans as a sacred medicine. They have used it extensively—its juice, its leaves, its roots, its (holy) smoke—to heal wounds and cure diseases, and in ceremonies of prayer and peace. And though the plant as most of us know it has been poisoned by chemicals and denatured by intensive mono-cropping and is therefore hardly the plant it was, still, to some modern Indians it remains a plant of positive power. I learned this when my Native American friends, Bill Wahpepah and his family, visited with me for a few days and the first thing he did was sow a few tobacco seeds in my garden.

Perhaps we can liberate tobacco from those who have captured and abused it, enslaving the plant on large plantations,

* Three months after reading this essay my daughter stopped smoking.

keeping it from freedom and its kin, and forcing it to enslave the world. Its true nature suppressed, no wonder it has become deadly. Maybe by sowing a few seeds of tobacco in our gardens and treating the plant with the reverence it deserves, we can redeem tobacco's soul and restore its self-respect.

Besides, how grim, if one is a smoker, to realize one is smoking a slave.

There is a slogan from a battered women's shelter that I especially like: "Peace on earth begins at home." I believe everything does. I think of a slogan for people trying to stop smoking: "Every home a smoke-free zone." Smoking is a form of self-battering that also batters those who must sit by, occasionally cajole or complain, and helplessly watch. I realize now that as a child I sat by, through the years, and literally watched my father kill himself: surely one such victory in my family, for the rich white men who own the tobacco companies, is enough.

1987

ON SEEING RED

[On January 19, 1984, more than 1,500 people gathered to see the West Coast premiere of the film *Seeing Red* at a benefit performance for *Socialist Review* and Democratic Socialists of America. This work by filmmakers Julia Reichert and Jim Klein depicts the history of the Communist party through interviews with rank-and-file CP members and former members. At the benefit, I read this as an introduction to the film.]

During the last years of the 1700s a black man in his sixties by the name of Benjamin Banneker helped survey the land and "run the lines" for what was to be the United States capital, Washington, D.C. He was acknowledged in his day, by Thomas Jefferson and others, as a remarkable mathematician, clock-maker (having made one of the first in America), surveyor, and astronomer, and the writer of precise, widely used almanacs that studied the stars and predicted the tides, eclipses of sun and moon, and all manner of natural phenomena. He was considered by many, then as now, to have been a genius.

Now this is more about Benjamin Banneker than most people know. It is certainly more than I knew growing up, or even until a few weeks ago. All I had was a vague notion that he had helped with the planning and laying out of Washington, D.C., and since I have usually only gone to Washington to demonstrate against something—often in horrendous weather—I thought little about it.

But isn't it strange, even astonishing, that a black man, born and raised in Maryland during the 1700s, a period of deepest enslavement of black people, was not only a free man all his life, but the son and grandson of free people as well, and all his life, furthermore, lived on his own sizable portion of excellent farmland? And isn't it odd that this man not only read and wrote (including several still-preserved *sharp* letters to a racist Thomas Jefferson), but also wrote, published, and distributed almanacs?

One night a few weeks ago, a friend of mine was reading to me from a book on Banneker's life* that he was studying for the purpose of understanding historical biography, and the first thing he read was about how Banneker had received much of his interest in, and knowledge about, the natural world from his grandmother, whose favorite grandchild he was, and who had been a farmer. She had encouraged his curiosity, supported his interests, taught him all she could, and loved him devoutly.

Aha, my friend and I thought, smiling knowingly at each other, the old black grandmother, who rarely gets any credit, surfaces again!

* *Your Most Humble Servant* by Shirley Graham (New York: Julian Messner, 1949).

A few pages later, however, this is what we found:

"The dark man's story had its beginnings nearly a hundred years before [he helped create our country's capital]. It started when a former English bondwoman, having served out her sentence, bought two male Africans off a slave ship just arrived at Maryland port. One of the Africans was [Banneker's] grandfather."

His grandmother was the former English bondwoman.

As it happened, Molly Walsh, Benjamin Banneker's English grandmother, had been accused of stealing a bucket of milk (which she said the cow she was milking kicked over) and had been sentenced to seven years of indentured servitude in a relatively new British colony, Maryland. When her time was served, she set off, barehanded, in a westerly direction into the wilderness, where she claimed a portion of unoccupied land (except by Indians and the Earth's natural animal and plant inhabitants: the layers of occupation are always thick) that lay surrounding a spring. She bartered with the Indians, and eventually she was able to purchase two slaves, who she hoped would clear the land for her. However, one of them, the son of a king in Africa, was forbidden by his station in life to work for anyone other than himself. This is the one, Bannaky (his African name), Molly Walsh married.

This interesting couple, who from all accounts were prosperous and happy, had four children. When the eldest daughter was old enough to marry, Molly Walsh again went down to the slave ships and bought an African. This man was Benjamin Banneker's father.

One day, in the parallel America we are constantly constructing alongside the one that is beginning to topple over, from its own distortions and lies, we will routinely have films about our real ancestors, not about the sanitized, error-free, unrecognizableas-human stereotypes we *endure*, for the most part, today. More and more the America that really exists and the Americans that really were and are will be acknowledged and studied. This is what so many of us, happy to count ourselves *alternative Americans* (to the ones in power or rampant on TV), work toward. For we know none of us can really feel good about our country or ourselves if we don't know who we are, where we've been or why, where we are going—and are afraid to guess.

Or, to quote Doris Lessing, "If we were able to describe [or see] ourselves accurately, we might be able to change."

One of the reasons our country seems so purposeless (except where making money is concerned) is that Americans, even (and perhaps especially) genetically, have been kept from acknowledging and being who they really are. There are few "white" people in America, for instance, and even fewer "black" ones. This reality is metaphor for countless other areas of delusion. In all our diversity we have been one people—just as the peoples of the world are one people—even when the most vicious laws of separation have forced us to believe we are not.

I, too, sing America.

Seeing Red is a film that reminds us not to despair of self-discovery of ourselves as a country. In it, some of our most radical political and *spirited* ancestors are recorded in all their dedication and complexity. Looking at and listening to them we see, many of us, that in our own beliefs and actions for a more just America (and world) we are only one of the many waves of movement for change, and that the American Communists of the first half of the twentieth century were an earlier wave for justice of which—whatever its failings and flaws—we can be proud. (Having numerous failings and flaws our own selves.)

Whenever I look at the city of Washington, D.C., now,

I know I will see superimposed on the phallic Washington Monument and the bunkered White House, the image of a small black boy with his hand tucked lovingly into his white grandmother's larger one. A founding couple to cheer the honest American heart. And when I study all the movements for justice that spring up and are battered, maligned, and sometimes destroyed by corrupt leaders and bad-faith followers, I will see the passion, devotion, disillusionment, and, finally, transcendence that mark the people in this film—who seem to have been made more whole by their struggles, rather than less.

These are some of the ancestors we have been encouraged to avoid, not to praise, not to know. This alone tells us much. In the America we are building, they laid many a foundation. In the America that will be, they have an honored place.

1984

JOURNAL

Ubud, Bali
February 12, 1987

Another rainy night. I am in bed, where I've been for several hours, after a long walk through Ubud to the monkey forest and then for lunch at the Lotus Café—entirely inhabited by Europeans and Americans and one stray very dark and pretty Indian girl in a vivid red dress. Then the walk home, stopping in a local shop—where the woman proprietor is sweet and sells wonderful flowing cool and colorful pants. (Rebecca, on seeing them hanging near the street, immediately exclaimed, "Miss Celie's pants!") Anyway, the pants I liked, knee length, with the flowing grace of a sarong, she no longer had, but she urged me to try a kind of flowered jumpsuit, very long—before she showed me how to adjust it to my shape—and Western-influenced Balinese. It looked great, so I bought it.

But the rain threatens to get me down. In the mornings there is a little sun—nothing direct; in the afternoons there are quite heavy showers, which, even if they are warm and we can walk right through them, I find a little overwhelming after the third or fourth day. Also feeling down because I've drunk so much beer, since the water is considered unsafe except here at the house. And, Robert says, this is the week before my period!

Anyway, *very* out of sorts, for me. It's true I overheard the housekeeper (who travels everywhere with an umbrella against rain and sun) tell Rebecca she "don't like black," as Rebecca was saying how much she wants to "brown"; and I resent always being perceived as just another "rich" American tourist and importuned to buy at every turn when we are walking and even here at the house. But Ubud is beautiful! I've never seen anything like it. The green rice paddies, the soft bluish-gray skies, the people who've created the landscape, and themselves, graceful, friendly, amazingly mellow.

So much so it is a shock to realize that as recently as 1965 more than 100,000 of them killed each other after an attempted Communist coup in Jakarta.

Bali makes me think of Uganda. The same gentle countryside and gentle people; the same massacres and blood baths.

Robert wondered aloud why you don't see middle-aged people, only the young and the old. A lot of them would have been among the 100,000.

I have many bites! The ones on my feet are especially maddening. In my gloomier moments this morning I thought: If it's going to rain all the time and I have to suffer mosquitoes as well, I might as well be in Mendocino. (Not knowing that Northern California was experiencing the worst flooding in thirty years!) I felt very homesick, which Rebecca found astonishing. She has taken to Bali—the people, the landscape, the food—

like the trouper she is. She is one of those old, old transparent souls the Universe radiates through without impediment, and so, wherever we go, within a week everyone seems aware of her presence. She walks in the rain as if it is sun.

Have been reading *Dancing in the Light*, by Shirley MacLaine; much of it is true, as I have experienced life, and a lot is straight Edgar Cayce. But it is sad to see her spirituality limited by her racialism. Indians and Africans have a hard time; especially Africans who, in one of her incarnations, frustrate her because they're not as advanced as she is! It is amusing to contemplate what the Africans must have thought of her.

But I don't care about any of this. In the kitchen, Ketut is making dinner, chicken satay. Rebecca and Robert are at a fire dance, to which I declined to go—pleading aching joints, footwear erosion, and mildew of the brain. The rain is coming down in torrents. Lightning is flashing. The house we've rented is spectacular: it faces a terraced hillside of rice paddies, two waterfalls, and coconut trees, and is built in Balinese style but is huge by Balinese standards, I think. Two large bedrooms downstairs and an open-air one upstairs, with another great wooden hand-carved antique Balinese bed at one end. The roof is thickly thatched.

Two days ago I celebrated my forty-second birthday here, with the two people I love most in the world; we talked about my visit, before we left home, to a very beautiful Indian woman guru, who spoke of the condition of "judness." A time of spiritual inertia, of feeling thick, heavy, devoid of light. Yet a good time, too, because, well, judness, too, is a part of life; and it is life itself that is good and holy. Not just the "dancing" times. Nor even the light.

Thinking of this, hoping my loved ones are dry, and smelling dinner, I look up straight into the eye of a giant red hibiscus flower Ketut just placed—with a pat on my head—by the bed. It says: Just *be*, Alice. Being is sufficient. Being is All. The cheerful, sunny self you are missing will return, as it always does, but only *being* will bring it back.

. . . .

NOT ONLY WILL YOUR TEACHERS APPEAR,

THEY WILL COOK NEW FOODS FOR YOU

My friends John and Eleanor founded the Mendocino Sea Vegetable Company a few years ago. They make their living harvesting seaweed—primarily nori, dulse, wakame, and sea-palm frond—on the Medocino coast at Elk beach, a small sheltered cove where a river meets the ocean, much loved by the locals, who not infrequently do sun and moon worship there. Large fires, lots of children, much to eat, and much gazing into the awesome heavens going *"um"* and (yes, still) "far *out.*"

When I first came to this area in the hills north of San Francisco, a friendly potter, from whom I bought dishes (now my friend Jan Wax), gave a party to which she invited all the people she knew whom she thought I'd like to meet. Among them were Eleanor and John, who, because it was potluck, brought their various concoctions of cooked and raw seaweed.

I tried hard to stay glued to the lasagne—which for a Southern-born person is exotic enough, but—

Try this, said Eleanor, offering a forkful of something that looked like chips of fried garbage bag.

Have a bit of that, said John, proffering something that didn't look any better.

Soon I was in the same fix I had found myself in when another new friend, at a similar gathering, pressed a fat wad of pig's-liver pâté into my hand while telling me in detail how she slaughtered the pig herself. *Where are the bushes around this house?* I'd wondered in panic, hastily muttering something about needing to go out and look at the stars, and attempting to chew.

The seaweed was *awful*, I thought. I didn't care how many minerals it had; besides, how positively gross that you could taste every one.

Excellent protein, said Eleanor.

No fat, said John.

All the trace elements your body's starved for, said my friend Jan, and a great cleanser of toxins (including nuclear) from the system. She gamely stuck a minuscule slice of something that looked unspeakable in her mouth.

I chewed on. It was kind of a cross between well-salted plastic or rubber and fish.

Have some of the soup, said Eleanor.

Try this dulse broth, said John.

They both had that soft-edged, gracefully aging hippie look that, unfortunately, evokes trust.

I didn't like the soup.

To hell, I thought, with the broth.

Over the months, at different potluck dinners, I sampled and nibbled the products of the Mendocino Sea Vegetable Company—"Grown Wild by the Pacific Ocean!" said their bags. Mainly I learned to hide when the deep-fried sea vegetable platter passed by.

But then, after about a year, two things happened.

One day Eleanor gave me a copy of their new sea vegetable cookbook* and at the same time cooked a new creation of hers called Navarro (after our small village, pop. 67) Oysters—because the seaweed, nori, in this instance, is rolled in beaten egg, whole-wheat flour, onion, and soy sauce, and looks and tastes something like oysters when it's cooked. Only, to my amazement, it tasted much better.

She cooked a bunch of "oysters" and served them over rice; we ate them with chopsticks. I ate more than anyone—in fact, every cell in my body seemed to wake up at the taste of this new treat, and after finishing the meal I experienced the most intense food satisfaction and well being that I'd ever had in my life.

During the coming ice age, which is probably already starting, people will need to get most of their vegetables from the sea, said John.

For the first time, this did not seem half bad.

They showed me the drying racks for the seaweed on a sunny hill behind their house, then gave me a large plastic garbage bag full of nori from the giant stash they kept in their bedroom prior to marketing. It was clear I was capable of becoming a nori freak.

For a summer my friend Robert and I ate Navarro Oysters several times a week. So did our guests. "*Ummm*," some said appreciatively. "Yuck! Where are the greens and corn bread?" muttered a few. But all were definitely up for this new experience.

And then one day John and Eleanor invited us to go harvesting with them. We left for the beach before sunup. When

---

* *Sea Vegetable (gourmet) Cookbook and Forager's Guide* by Eleanor and John Lewallen (Navarro, CA: The Mendocino Sea Vegetable Company, 1983).

we arrived, the tide was out. We clambered over the rocks, marveling at the beauty of the seaweed; its shimmery iridescence as the sun revealed its purples, greens, browns, yellows, and blues. We picked and we picked, always careful to leave enough to grow. Bags of seaweed. Then we explored the rocks beyond the beach, where I promptly slipped and fell, over my head, into the water. Then we lay in the sun to dry, thankful for the ocean's generosity, its cleanliness, and its peace.

Now the U.S. government is planning to lease Mendocino offshore drilling rights to the oil companies, although oil drilling will tar the beach, pollute the air, and contaminate and possibly kill marine creatures and seaweed. John and Eleanor's livelihood is threatened. Many of the people who live here and love the ocean are heartsick and outraged. Petitions against drilling are flying thick and fast, John and Eleanor generating some of them—with a little help from their friends, who remember their teachings:

If you eat more sea vegetables, you can eat less meat.

If you eat less meat, farmers can grow more grains and beans.

Everyone knows if we eat mainly grains and beans it is easily possible to feed everyone on the planet.

And there's always the next ice age to consider.

I feel as if my very right to grow in new ways that protect and nurture the planet is being threatened by the government's plan. How cruel, too, eventually to learn a better way of doing something and then be denied the use of it. It is like the reactionary laws our government sometimes enacts that take away freedoms from people—women, gays, people of color, children—that much of the rest of the population has learned to be glad they have, because they understand this ultimately means a richer, freer life for themselves. Freedom, after all, is like love: the more you give to others, the more you have.

Every small, positive change we can make in ourselves repays us in confidence in the future. I am happy to say that, thanks to the persistence of my friends, I have changed about seaweed. From someone who hid behind the hostess when the fried wakame platter went by, I've become someone who doesn't bother to take food to the beach. I can lie on the sand in the sun and eat the dried seaweed straight off the rocks.

1986

• • • • • • • • • • •

EVERYTHING IS A HUMAN BEING

[This was written to celebrate the birth of Martin Luther King, Jr., and delivered as a keynote address at the University of California, Davis, January 15, 1983.]

• • •

. . . There are people who think that only people have emotions like pride, fear, and joy, but those who know will tell you all things are alive, perhaps not in the same way we are alive, but each in its own way, as should be, for we are not all the same. And though different from us in shape and life span, different in Time and Knowing, yet are trees alive. And rocks. And water. And all know emotion.

—Anne Cameron, DAUGHTERS OF COPPER WOMAN*

• • •

* Vancouver: Press Gang, 1981.

Some years ago a friend and I walked out into the countryside
to listen to what the Earth was saying, and to better hear our
own thoughts. We had prepared ourselves to experience what
in the old days would have been called a vision, and what today
probably has no name that is not found somewhat amusing by
many. Because there is no longer countryside that is not owned
by someone, we stopped at the entrance to a large park, many
miles distant from the city. By the time we had walked a hundred
yards, I felt I could go no farther and lay myself down where I
was, across the path in a grove of trees. For several hours I lay
there, and other people entering the park had to walk around
me. But I was hardly aware of them. I was in intense dialogue
with the trees.

As I was lying there, really across their feet, I felt or "heard"
with my feelings the distinct request from them that I remove
myself. But these are not feet, I thought, peering at them closely,
but roots. Roots do not tell you to go away. It was then that I
looked up and around me into the "faces." These "faces" were
all middle-aged to old conifers, and they were all suffering from
some kind of disease, the most obvious sign of which was a light
green fungus, resembling moss and lichen, that nearly covered
them, giving them—in spite of the bright spring sunlight—an
eerie, fantastical aspect. Beneath this greenish envelopment,
the limbs of the trees, the "arms," were bent in hundreds of
shapes in a profusion of deformity. Indeed, the trees reminded
me of nothing so much as badly rheumatoid elderly people, as
I began to realize how difficult, given their bent shapes, it would
be for their limbs to move freely in the breeze. Clearly these
were sick people, or trees; irritable, angry, and growing old in
pain. And they did not want me lying on their gnarled and no
doubt aching feet.

Looking again at their feet, or roots—which stuck up all
over the ground and directly beneath my cheek—I saw that the

ground from which they emerged was gray and dead-looking, as if it had been poisoned. Aha, I thought, this is obviously a place where chemicals were dumped. The soil has been poisoned, the trees afflicted, slowly dying, and they do not like it. I hastily communicated this deduction to the trees and asked that they understand it was not *I* who had done this. I just moved to this part of the country, I said. But they were not appeased. Get up. Go away, they replied. But I refused to move. Nor could I. I needed to make them agree to my innocence.

The summer before this encounter I lived in the northern hills of California, where much logging is done. Each day on the highway, as I went to buy groceries or to the river to swim, I saw the loggers' trucks, like enormous hearses, carrying the battered bodies of the old sisters and brothers, as I thought of them, down to the lumberyards in the valley. In fact, this sight, in an otherwise peaceful setting, distressed me—as if I lived in a beautiful neighborhood that daily lost hundreds of its finest members, while I sat mournful but impotent beside the avenue that carried them away.

It was of this endless funeral procession that I thought as I lay across the feet of the sick old relatives whose "safe" existence in a public park (away from the logging trucks) had not kept them safe at all.

I *love* trees, I said.

Human, *please*, they replied.

But I do not cut you down in the prime of life. I do not haul your mutilated and stripped bodies shamelessly down the highway. It is the lumber companies, I said.

Just go away, said the trees.

All my life you have meant a lot to me, I said. I love your grace, your dignity, your serenity, your generosity . . .

Well, said the trees, before I actually finished this list, we find you without grace, without dignity, without serenity, and there is no generosity in you either—just ask any tree. You butcher us, you burn us, you grow us only to destroy us. Even when we grow ourselves, you kill us, or cut off our limbs. That we are alive and have feelings means nothing to you.

But *I*, as an individual, am innocent, I said. Though it did occur to me that I live in a wood house, I eat on a wood table, I sleep on a wood bed.

My uses of wood are modest, I said, and always tailored to my needs. I do not slash through whole forests, destroying hundreds of trees in the process of "harvesting" a few.

But finally, after much discourse, I understood what the trees were telling me: Being an individual doesn't matter. Just as human beings perceive all trees as one (didn't a U.S. official say recently that "when you've seen one tree, you've seen 'em all"?), all human beings, to the trees, are one. We are judged by our worst collective behavior, since it is so vast; not by our singular best. The Earth holds us responsible for our crimes against it, not as individuals, but as a species—this was the message of the trees. I found it to be a terrifying thought. For I had assumed that the Earth, the spirit of the Earth, noticed exceptions—those who wantonly damage it and those who do not. But the Earth is wise. It has given itself into the keeping of all, and all are therefore accountable.

And how hard it will be to change our worst behavior!

Last spring I moved even deeper into the country, and went eagerly up the hill from my cabin to start a new garden. As I was patting the soil around the root of a new tomato plant, I awakened a small garden snake who lived in the tomato bed. Though panicked and not knowing at the time what kind of snake it was, I tried calmly to direct it out of the garden, now that I, a human being, had arrived to take possession of it. It went. The next day, however, because the tomato bed *was* its home, the snake came back. Once more I directed it away. The third time it came back, I called a friend—who thought I was badly frightened, from my nervous behavior—and he killed it. It looked very small and harmless, hanging from the end of his hoe.

Everything I was ever taught about snakes—that they are dangerous, frightful, repulsive, sinister—went into the murder of this snake person, who was only, after all, trying to remain in his or her home, perhaps the only home he or she had ever known. Even my ladylike "nervousness" in its presence was learned behavior. I knew at once that killing the snake was not the first act that should have occurred in my new garden, and I grieved that I had apparently learned nothing, as a human being, since the days of Adam and Eve.

Even on a practical level, killing this small, no doubt bewildered and disoriented creature made poor sense, because throughout the summer snakes just like it regularly visited the garden (and deer, by the way, ate all the tomatoes), so that it appeared to me that the little snake I killed was always with me. Occasionally a very large mama or papa snake wandered into the cabin yard, as if to let me know its child had been murdered, and it knew who was responsible for it.

These garden snakes, said my neighbors, are harmless; they eat mice and other pests that invade the garden. In this respect, they are even helpful to humans. And yet, I am still afraid of them, because that is how I was taught to be. Deep in the psyche of most of us there is this fear—and long ago, I do not doubt, in the psyche of ancient peoples, there was a similar fear of trees. And of course a fear of other human beings, for that is where all fear of natural things leads us: to fear of ourselves, fear of each other, and fear even of the spirit of the Universe, because out of fear we often greet its outrageousness with murder.

That fall, they say, the last of the bison herds was slaughtered by the Wasichus.* I can remember when the bison were so many that they could not be counted, but more and more Wasichus came to kill them until there were only heaps of bones scattered where they used to be. The Wasichus did not kill them to eat; they killed them for the metal that makes them crazy, and they took only the hides to sell. Sometimes they did not even take the hides, only the tongues; and I have heard that fire-boats came down the Missouri River loaded with dried bison tongues. You can see that the men who did this were crazy. Sometimes they did not even take the tongues; they just killed and killed because they liked to do that. When we hunted bison, we killed only what we needed. And when there was nothing left but heaps of bones, the Wasichus came and gathered up even the bones and sold them.

—BLACK ELK SPEAKS†

In this way, the Wasichus starved the Indians into submission, and forced them to live on impoverished "reservations" in their own land. Like the little snake in my garden, many of the Indians returned again and again to their ancient homes and hunting grounds, only to be driven off with greater and greater brutality until they were broken or killed.

The Wasichus in Washington who ordered the slaughter of bison and Indian and those on the prairies who did the deed are frequently thought of, by some of us, as "fathers of our

* Wasichu was a term used by the Oglala Sioux to designate the white man, but it had no reference to the color of his skin. It means: He who takes the fat. It is possible to be white and not a Wasichu or to be a Wasichu and not white. In the United States, historically speaking, Wasichus of color have usually been in the employ of the military, which is the essence of Wasichu.

† By John G. Neihardt (New York: William Morrow, 1932).

country," along with the Indian killers and slave owners Washington and Jefferson and the like.

Yet what "father" would needlessly exterminate any of his children?

Are not the "fathers," rather, those Native Americans, those "wild Indians" like Black Elk, who said, "It is the story of all life that is holy and is good to tell, and of us two-leggeds sharing in it with the four-leggeds and the wings of the air and all green things; for these are children of one mother and their father is one Spirit"?

Indeed, America, the country, acts so badly, so much like a spoiled adolescent boy, because it has never acknowledged the "fathers" that existed before the "fathers" of its own creation. It has been led instead—in every period of its brief and troubled history—by someone who might be called Younger Brother (after the character in E. L. Doctorow's novel *Ragtime*, set in turn-of-the-century America), who occasionally blunders into good and useful deeds, but on the whole never escapes from the white Victorian house of racist and sexist repression, puritanism, and greed.

The Wasichu speaks, in all his U.S. history books, of "opening up virgin lands." Yet there were people living here, on "Turtle Island," as the Indians called it, for thousands of years; but living so gently on the land that to Wasichu eyes it looked untouched. Yes, it was "still," as they wrote over and over again, with lust, "virginal." If it were a bride, the Wasichus would have permitted it to wear a white dress. For centuries on end Native Americans lived on the land, making love to it through worship and praise, without once raping or defiling it. The Wasichus—who might have chosen to imitate the Indians, but didn't because to them the *Indians* were savages—have been raping and defiling it since the day they came. It is ironic to think that if the Indians who were here then "discovered" America as it is now, they would find little reason to want to stay. This is a fabulous *land*, not because it is a country, but because it is soaked in so many years of love. And though the Native Americans fought as much as any other people among themselves (much to their loss!), never did they fight against the earth, which they correctly perceived as their mother, or against their father, the sky, now thought of mainly as "outer space," where primarily bigger and "better" wars have a projected future.

The Wasichus may be fathers of the country, but the Native Americans, the Indians, are the parents ("guardians," as they've always said they are) of the land.* And, in my opinion, as Earthling above all, we must get to know these parents "from our mother's side" before it is too late. It has been proved that the land can exist without the country—and be better for it; it has not been proved (though some space enthusiasts appear to think so) that the country can exist without the land. And the land is being killed.

Sometimes when I teach, I try to help my students understand what it must feel like to be a slave. Not many of them can go to South Africa and ask the black people enslaved by the Wasichus there, or visit the migrant-labor camps kept hidden from their neighborhoods, so we talk about slavery as it existed in America, a little over a hundred years ago. One day I asked if any of them felt they had been treated "like dirt." No; many of them felt they had been treated badly at some time in their lives (they were largely middle class and white) but no one felt

---

* Though much of what we know of our Indian ancestors concerns the male, it is good to remember who produced him; that women in some tribes were shamans, could vote, and among the Onondaga still elect the men who lead the tribe. And, inasmuch as "women's work" has always involved cleaning up after the young, as well as teaching them principles by which to live, we have our Indian female parent to thank for her care of Turtle Island, as well as the better documented male who took her instructions so utterly to heart.

he or she had been treated like dirt. Yet what pollution you breathe, I pointed out, which the atmosphere also breathes; what a vast number of poisons you eat with your food, which the Earth has eaten just before you. How unexpectedly many of you will fall ill and die from cancer because the very ground on which you build your homes will be carcinogenic. As the Earth is treated "like dirt"—its dignity demeaned by wanton dumpings of lethal materials all across its proud face and in its crystal seas—so are we all treated.

Some of us have become used to thinking that woman is the nigger of the world, that a person of color is the nigger of the world, that a poor person is the nigger of the world. But, in truth, Earth itself has become the nigger of the world. It is perceived, ironically, as other, alien, evil, and threatening by those who are finding they cannot draw a healthful breath without its cooperation. While the Earth is poisoned, everything it supports is poisoned. While the Earth is enslaved, none of us is free. While the Earth is "a nigger," it has no choice but to think of us all as Wasichus. While it is "treated like dirt," so are we.

In this time, when human life—because of human greed, avarice, ignorance, and fear—hangs by a thread, it is of disarmament that every thoughtful person thinks; for regardless of whether we all agree that we deserve to live, or not, as a species, most of us have the desire. But disarmament must also occur in the heart and in the spirit. We must absolutely reject the way of the Wasichu that we are so disastrously traveling, the way that respects most (above nature, obviously above life itself, above even the spirit of the Universe) the "metal that makes men crazy." The United States, the country, has no doubt damned its soul because of how it has treated others, and if it is true that we reap what we sow, as a country we have only to recognize the poison inside us as the poison we forced others to drink. But the land is innocent. It is still Turtle Island, and more connected to the rest of the Universe than to the United States government. It is beginning to throw up the poisons it has been forced to drink, and we must help it by letting go of our own; for until it is healthy and well, we cannot be.

Our primary connection is to the Earth, our mother and father; regardless of who "owns" pieces and parts, we, as sister and brother beings to the "four-leggeds (and the fishes) and the wings of the air," share the whole. No one should be permitted to buy a part of our Earth to dump poisons in, just as we would not sell one of our legs to be used as a trash can.

Many of us are afraid to abandon the way of the Wasichu because we have become addicted to his way of death. The Wasichu has promised us so many good things, and has actually delivered several. But "progress," once claimed by the present chief of the Wasichus to be their "most important product," has meant hunger, misery, enslavement, unemployment, and worse to millions of people on the globe. The many time-saving devices we have become addicted to, because of our "progress," have freed us to watch endless reruns of commercials, sitcoms, and murders.

Our thoughts must be on how to restore to the Earth its dignity as a living being; how to stop raping and plundering it as a matter of course. We must begin to develop the consciousness that everything has equal rights because existence itself is equal. In other words, we are all here: trees, people, snakes, alike. We must realize that even tiny insects in the South American jungle know how to make plastic, for instance; they have simply chosen not to cover the Earth with it. The Wasichu's uniqueness is not his ability to "think" and "invent"—from the evidence, almost everything does this in some fashion or other—it is his profound unnaturalness. His lack of harmony with other peoples and places, and with the very environment to which he owes his life.

In James Mooney's *Myths of the Cherokee and Sacred Formulas of the Cherokees,* collected between 1887 and 1890, he relates many interesting practices of the original inhabitants of this land, among them the custom of asking pardon of slain or offended animals. And in writing about the needless murder of the snake who inhabited our garden—the snake's and mine— I ask its pardon and, in the telling of its death, hope to save the lives of many of its kin.

> The missionary Washburn [says Mooney] tells how among the Cherokees of Arkansas, he was once riding along, accompanied by an Indian on foot, when they discovered a poisonous snake coiled beside the path. "I observed Blanket turned aside to avoid the serpent, but made no sign of attack, and I requested the interpreter to get down and kill it. He did so, and I then inquired of Blanket why he did not kill the serpent. He answered, 'I never kill snakes and so snakes never kill me.' "
>
> The trader Henry [Mooney observes elsewhere] tells of similar behavior among the Objibwa of Lake Superior in 1764. While gathering wood he was startled by a sudden rattle. . . . "I no sooner saw the snake, than I hastened to the canoe, in order to procure my gun; but, the Indians observing what I was doing, inquired the occasion, and being informed, begged me to desist. At the same time, they followed me to the spot, with their pipes and tobacco pouches in their hands. On returning, I found the snake still coiled.
>
> "The Indians, on their part, surrounded it, all addressing

it by turns, and calling it their *grandfather*; but yet keeping at some distance. During this part of the ceremony, they filled their pipes; and now each blew the smoke toward the snake, who, as it appeared to me, really received it with pleasure. In a word, after remaining coiled, and receiving incense, for the space of half an hour, it stretched itself along the ground, in visible good humor. Its length was between four and five feet. Having remained outstretched for some time, at last it moved slowly away, the Indians following it, and still addressing it by the title of grandfather, beseeching it to take care of their families during their absence, and to be pleased to open the heart of Sir William Johnson (the British Indian Agent, whom they were about to visit) so that he might *show them charity*, and fill their canoe with rum. One of the chiefs added a petition, that the snake would take no notice of the insult which had been offered by the Englishman, who would even have put him to death, but for the interference of the Indians, to whom it was hoped he would impute no part of the offense. They further requested, that he would remain, and inhabit their country, and not return among the English. . . ."

What makes this remarkable tale more so is that the "bite" of the Englishman's rum was to afflict the Indians far more severely than the bite of any tremendous number of poisonous snakes.

That the Indians were often sexist, prone to war, humanly flawed, I do not dispute. It is their light step upon the Earth that I admire and would have us emulate. The new way to exist on the Earth may well be the ancient way of the steadfast lovers of this particular land. No one has better appreciated Earth than the Native American. Whereas to the Wasichus only the white male attains full human status, everything to the Indian was a relative. Everything was a human being.

As I finish writing this, I notice a large spider sleeping underneath my desk. It does not look like me. It is a different size. But that it loves life as I do, I have no doubt. It is something to think about as I study its many strange but oddly beautiful dozen or so legs, its glowing coral-and-amber coloring, its thick web, whose intricate pattern I would never be able to duplicate. Imagine building your house from your own spit!

In its modesty, its fine artistry and self-respecting competency, is it not like some gay, independent person many of us have known? Perhaps a rule for permissible murder should be that beyond feeding and clothing and sheltering ourselves, even abundantly, we should be allowed to destroy only what we ourselves can re-create. We cannot re-create this world. We cannot re-create "wilderness." We cannot even, truly, re-create ourselves. Only our behavior can we re-create, or create anew.

> Hear me, four quarters of the world—a relative I am! Give me the strength to walk the soft earth, a relative to all that is! Give me the eyes to see and the strength to understand, that I may be like you. . . .
>
> Great Spirit, Great Spirit, my Grandfather, all over the earth the faces of living things are all alike. With tenderness have these come up out of the ground. Look upon these faces of children without number and with children in their arms, that they may face the winds and walk the good road to the day of quiet.
>
> —BLACK ELK SPEAKS

Note

The Onondagas are the "Keepers of the Fire" of the Six Nation Confederacy in New York state. The Confederacy (originally composed of five nations) is perhaps the oldest democratic union of nations in the Western world, dating back roughly to the time of the Magna Carta. It is governed under an ancient set of principles known as the "Gayaneshakgowa," or Great Law of Peace, which in written form is the constitution of the Six Nation Confederacy.

This remarkable document contains what well may have been the first detailed pronouncements on democratic popular elections, the consent of the governed, the need to monitor and approve the behavior of governmental leaders, the importance of public opinion, the rights of women, guarantees of free speech and religion, and the equitable distribution of wealth.

Benjamin Franklin and Thomas Jefferson acknowledged in the mid-18th century that their own ideas for a democratic confederacy were based largely on what they had learned from the Six Nations. A century later Friedrich Engels paid a similar tribute to the Great Law of Peace while making his contribution to the theory of Marxism.

—*Jon Stewart*, Pacific News Service

•　　•　　•　　•　　•　　•　　•　　•

"NOBODY WAS SUPPOSED TO SURVIVE":

THE MOVE MASSACRE

Under questioning by commission members, Mr. Goode said he thought he managed the crisis well with the information he had at the time. But he said that he realized in retrospect that his subordinates had not given him enough data to make proper decisions, such as dropping a bomb on the MOVE house. *He was first asked for permission, which he granted, to use the device 17 minutes before it was dropped from a helicopter.* . . . Mr. Goode also said that Mr. Sambor had violated his order not to involve police officers in the assault who might hold what the Mayor called a "grudge" from participating in a confrontation with the radical group at another MOVE house in 1978. *Several officers involved in that siege participated in the assault this year.* [My italics.]
—NEW YORK TIMES, *Oct. 16, 1985*

One of two people known to have survived an inferno that killed 11 people said that police gunfire drove fleeing members of the radical group MOVE back into their blazing house in the May 13 confrontation with police. . . .
—NEW YORK TIMES, *Oct. 31, 1985*

[Detective] Stephenson's log also gives a gruesome glimpse of just what kind of deaths MOVE was forced to endure. Excerpts of entries concerning the search for bodies revealed, "15:35—The body of a female was recovered 10 feet from rear door, 8 feet from west wall. On her foot, left, was a black Chinese slipper and was lying on her right side facing the rear wall. No other clothing . . . head and chest appeared to be crushed, can't recall hair—all photographed.

"16:05—The body of a child was recovered under the female. Same area. No description. Only bones.

"17:50—Left forearm with clenched fist recovered at door. . . .

"19:45—Adult male from waist down recovered, no descriptions. Some skin. . . .

"11:30—The body of one Negro/male was lifted from the front area with his heart outside the chest area by crane . . . no arms, legs missing from thighs down. No head. . . ."
—REVOLUTIONARY WORKER, *Nov. 14, 1985*

According to the report [The Commission on the MOVE "confrontation"], *Goode paused only 30 seconds before approving the dropping of the explosives.* [My italics.]

Negotiation with MOVE was never seriously considered. . . .

A long gun battle ensued. The commission says the

10,000 rounds of ammunition fired by police was "excessive and unreasonable," especially given the presence of children in the residence.

In addition, the report notes that work crews found only two pistols, a shotgun and a .22-caliber rifle in the rubble of the MOVE compound. . . .

Once the fire began, it could have been quickly put out if the Fire Department immediately had used two high pressure Squrt [*sic*] water guns it had trained on the house. However . . . Sambor and Fire Commissioner William C. Richmond hastily made the "unconscionable" decision to let the fire burn, hoping to force the MOVE members to flee. . . .

At least two adults and four children attempted to escape after the house caught fire, but police gunfire prevented them from fleeing.
—THE PHILADELPHIA INQUIRER, *Mar. 2, 1986*

Nobody was supposed to survive.
—*Ramona Africa,*
NEW YORK TIMES, *January 7, 1986*

I was in Paris in mid-May of 1985 when I heard the news about MOVE. My traveling companion read aloud the item in the newspaper that described the assault on a house on Osage Avenue in Philadelphia occupied by a group of "radical, black, back-to-nature" revolutionaries that local authorities had been "battling" for over a decade. As he read the article detailing the attack that led, eventually, to the actual bombing of the house (with military bombing material supplied to local police by the FBI) and the deaths of at least eleven people, many of them women, five of them children, our mutual feeling was of horror, followed immediately by anger and grief. Grief: that feeling of unassuageable sadness and rage that makes the heart feel naked to the elements, clawed by talons of ice. For, even knowing nothing of MOVE (short for Movement, which a revolution assumes) and little of the "City of Brotherly Love," Philadelphia, we recognized the heartlessness of the crime, and realized that for the local authorities to go after eleven people, five of them children, with the kind of viciousness and force usually reserved for war, what they were trying to kill had to be more than the human beings involved; it had to be a spirit, an idea.

But what spirit? What idea?

There was only one adult survivor of the massacre: a young black woman named Ramona Africa. She suffered serious burns over much of her body (and would claim, later in court, as she sustained her own defense: "I am guilty of nothing but hiding in the basement trying to protect myself and . . . MOVE children"). The bombing of the MOVE house ignited a fire that roared through the black, middle-class neighborhood, totally destroying more than sixty houses and leaving 250 people homeless.

There we stood on a street corner in Paris, reading between the lines. It seems MOVE people never combed their hair, but wore it in long "ropes" that people assumed was unclean. Since this is also how we wear our hair, we recognized this "weird" style: dreadlocks. The style of the ancients: Ethiopians and Egyptians. Easily washed, quickly dried—a true wash-and-wear style for black people (and adventuresome whites) and painless, which is no doubt why MOVE people chose it for their children. And for themselves: "Why suffer for cosmetic reasons?" they must have asked.

It appeared that the MOVE people were vegetarians and ate their food raw because they believed raw food healthier for the body and the soul. They believed in letting orange peels, banana peels, and other organic refuse "cycle" back into the earth. Composting? They did not believe in embalming dead people or burying them in caskets. They thought they should be allowed to "cycle" back to the earth, too. They loved dogs (their leader, John Africa, was called "The Dog Man" because he cared for so many) and never killed animals of any kind, not even rats (which infuriated their neighbors), because they believed in the sanctity of all life.

Hmmm.

Further: They refused to send their children to school, fearing drugs and an indoctrination into the sickness of American life. They taught them to enjoy "natural" games, in the belief that games based on such figures as Darth Vader caused "distortions" in the personalities of the young that inhibited healthy, spontaneous expression. They exercised religiously, running miles every day with their dogs, rarely had sit-down dinners, ate out of big sacks of food whenever they were hungry, owned no furniture except a few pieces they'd found on the street, and refused to let their children wear diapers because of the belief that a free bottom is healthier. They abhorred the use of plastic. They enjoyed, apparently, the use of verbal profanity, which they claimed lost any degree of profanity when placed next to atomic or nuclear weapons of any sort, which they considered *really* profane. They hated the police, who they claimed harassed them relentlessly (a shoot-out with police in 1978 resulted in the death of one officer and the imprisonment of several MOVE people). They occasionally self-righteously and disruptively harangued their neighbors, using bullhorns. They taught anyone who would listen that the U.S. political and social system is corrupt to the core—and tried to be, themselves, a different tribe within it.

Back home I heard little of the MOVE massacre. Like members of MOVE, I don't watch TV. The local papers were full of bombings, as usual, but bombings in Libya, Lebanon,

El Salvador, Angola, and Mozambique. There seemed to be an amazingly silent response, outside of Philadelphia,* to the bombing of these black people, the majority of them women and children, presided over, after all, by a black mayor, the Honorable Wilson Goode of the aforementioned City of Brotherly etcetera. (Meanwhile, there was incredible controversy over the filming of a movie in which no one is killed and a black man abuses a woman!†) Nor do I yet know what to make of this silence. Was the bombing of black people, with a black person ostensibly (in any case) responsible, too much for the collective black psyche to bear? Were people stunned by the realization that such an atrocity—formerly confined to Libya or Vietnam—could happen to us? Did I simply miss the controversy? Were there town meetings and teach-ins and pickets round the clock in every city in which Wilson Goode and his police officers appeared? Or did the media (and Philadelphia officials, including the black mayor of which black Philadelphians were so proud) succeed in convincing the public that the victims were indeed the aggressors and deserved what they got? Ramona Africa, after all, was arrested for assault and sentenced to prison for "riot"—and it was *her* house that was bombed, her friends, colleagues, and loved ones who were slaughtered.

Thumbing through the stacks of articles I've been sent on the MOVE massacre I see that an earlier assault on their house occurred in 1978, when a white man, Frank Rizzo, was mayor. Under Rizzo, MOVE people were evicted, often imprisoned, and their house was eventually razed. Under Goode, their house

---

* For several weeks the Philadelphia Special Investigation Commission, appointed by Goode, conducted hearings, in an apparent attempt to justify the massacre and exonerate the police and the mayor himself.
† *The Color Purple.*

was bombed, their neighborhood destroyed, and many of them killed. And why?

Through both administrations, the city officials and MOVE neighbors appeared to have one thing in common: a hatred of the way MOVE people chose to live. They didn't like the "stench" of people who refused, because they believe chemicals cause cancer, to use deodorant; didn't like orange peels and watermelon rinds on the ground; didn't like all those "naked" children running around with all that uncombed hair. They didn't appreciate the dogs and the rats. They thought the children should be in school and that the adults and children should eat cooked food; everybody should eat meat. They probably thought it low class that in order to make money MOVE people washed cars and shoveled snow. And appeared to enjoy it.

MOVE people were not middle class. Many of them were high-school dropouts. Many of them were mothers without husbands. Or young men who refused any inducement to "fit in." Yet they had the nerve to critique the system. To reject it and to set up, in place of its rules, guidelines for living that reflected their own beliefs.

The people of MOVE are proof that poor people, not just upper- and middle-class whites and blacks who become hippies, are capable of intelligently perceiving and analyzing American life, politically and socially, and of devising and attempting to follow a different—and, to them, better—way. But because they are poor and black, this is not acceptable behavior to middle-class whites and blacks who think all poor black people should be happy with jherri curls, mindless (and lying) TV shows, and Kentucky fried chicken.

This is not to condone the yelping of fifty to sixty dogs in the middle of the night, dogs MOVE people rescued from the streets (and probable subsequent torture in "scientific" labora-

tories), fed, and permitted to sleep in their house. Nor to con-
done the bullhorn they used to air their neighbors' "backward-
ness" or political transgressions, as apparently they had a bad
habit of doing. From what I read, MOVE people were more
fanatical than the average neighbors. I probably would not have
been able to live next door to them for a day.

The question is: Did they deserve the harassment, abuse,
and, finally, the vicious death other people's intolerance of their
life style brought upon them? *Every bomb ever made falls on
all of us*. And the answer is: No.

The real reason for the government hit-squad is no secret:
MOVE is an organization of radical utopians. Their po-
litical activity, their allusions to Africa, their dreadlocks,
all speak rejection of the system. For this, they have been
harassed, besieged, framed, beaten, shot, jailed, and now
bombed. The reported shout from the MOVE compound
this last fateful Monday was: "We ain't got a fucking thing
to lose."*

How does it feel
to watch your neighbors
burn to death
because you hated
the sound
of their dogs
barking
and were not yourself
crazy
about compost heaps?

* Carl Dix, *Revolutionary Worker* leaflet, May 16, 1985.

How does it feel
to hear the children
scream in the flames
because you said
the clothes they wore
in winter
were never enough
to keep them warm?

How does it feel
to know the hair
you hated
spreads like a fan
around a severed head
beside the door?

How does it feel
to "take full responsibility,"
as the mayor said,
for an "absolute
disaster"
to your soul?

How does it feel to massacre
the part of yourself
that is really,
well—
considering the nappy hair
    and watermelon rinds
and naked black booties
and all—
pretty much
an embarrassment?

What *will* the white people
think!

How does it feel, folks?
The bad image is gone:
you can talk now.
How does it feel?

When they come for us
what can we say?

Our beliefs are
our country.
Our hair is
our flag.
Our love of ourselves
is our freedom.

We, too, fucking yes,
sing America.

1986

ALL THE BEARDED IRISES OF LIFE:

CONFESSIONS OF A HOMOSPIRITUAL

I was an adult before I realized that when I was growing up in the fifties in a small segregated town in the South there were at least three groups of people I never saw—people who were present in the life of the town, in the culture and activities of the two obvious (black and white) communities, but camouflaged: Jews, who were few in any event and were blended into the white community (at least from a black person's perspective); Indians, who were racially blended into both black and white communities (heavily so, in the black community); and homosexuals, who were blended into the heterosexual world of both. I have no memory, as a child, of ever seeing, hearing about, or even being able to imagine homosexuality.

Even in college there were only jokes I didn't get about "queers," and, on return trips home, whispers that such-and-such a one was "funny." The social taboo of my college years, of which I *was* aware, was interracialism. I actively combatted it by having numerous friendships with white women and children, and by dating white men. I later married, had a child by, and divorced a white man.

It was through erotica that I first understood that two women or two men could be sexually attracted to each other. I was staying in the borrowed rooms of a former college classmate, and she had books that graphically described methods of attaining orgasm. Some of these methods were very strange. One of them I'll never forget described the languid inventiveness of a young woman guest at a boring dinner party, who masturbated herself—underneath the table and while ostensibly listening to the tiresome monologue of her host—with a fork. She was actually gazing at the woman across the table from her at the time. This seemed to me wonderfully different from the usual story of "boy meets girl." But why a fork? Use of this utensil was a bit decadent, I felt. Not to mention cold.

My adult awareness of homosexuality comes from my own feelings of attraction to other women as well as to men (and to yellow people, red people, brown, and white people, in addition to the prescribed black ones). But these feelings toward women, as toward people of other races, were buried very deep, so deep, in fact, that I was friends for many years with a woman with whom I discussed everything, who actually had women lovers, but we never discussed that. It was my fault, I'm sure, that we didn't. I was married, I was obviously attracted to men. For that is one of the things, for a woman, that marriage is supposed to "prove." I never spoke of women sexually. It never even occurred to me. Saying the word "lesbian" caused me to stammer.

Yet my friend's refusal to reveal the lesbian side of her nature, surely her most instrinsic self, in a friendship in which everything else was shared—including my struggles in loving men—hurt me deeply. I assumed it meant lack of trust. It certainly indicated fear of me, as a nonlesbian. Fear that I would betray her. That I would not be someone to be counted on. That I would not understand. I was insulted by this. (Aquarians, they say, can tolerate anything but being thought narrow-minded. In my case, this is certainly true.)

My indignation at this lack of faith in me, however, was the cosmic slap I needed to begin to see what was before my eyes and to begin to hear, in conversations with both women and men, the very obvious things that were or were not said. I began to be able to see and hear through the camouflage, and many new and interesting worlds emerged.

After one fully completed lifetime of work, marriage, and loves in the Northeast and the South and over a decade after college, I arrived in San Francisco, ready for anything, but in fact deeply in love with—as I thought of it, sometimes wearily— yet another man. Or, as I also sometimes put it, "with my *last* man!" For I faced the dilemma of the consciousness-raised woman who is appalled to realize that even after knowing "the worst" about men in general one is still very attracted, often, to individual men. (In order to comprehend quickly that this is not necessarily hypocritical, think of how you feel about white people collectively, then think about your white friends. If you are white, think about blacks. . . .) I wanted very much for my lesbian friends—of whom I now had several—to accept me and my choice of partners, as I accepted them and theirs. In fact, and to complicate matters in what I thought was a rather beautiful way, this was also a need shared by my lover, the "last man." Far from feeling threatened by my lesbian friends or even by his own, he admired them. He liked the same things I liked: their independence and courage, their pride in self-sufficiency and competence, their refusal to be dominated by men, their love, erotic and platonic, for other women. He was also a great admirer of their clothes.

It was no mystery to either of us—observing heterosexual relationships every day in which women are oppressed or routinely denied the full expression of who they are simply because of their gender—why women who wished to do so were right to choose other women as lovers. Also, in themselves, women are beautiful and lovable. Yet, because my lover and I were with each other, we were assumed by our more radical lesbian friends to be oblivious of this, and from time to time we agreed that he should not be present when these friends came to call. But this was painful for us to accept, even though we understood. However, having lived through the black separatist movement, we *did* understand. But, come to think of it, we'd both been hurt then, too.

In any case, I was not, unfortunately (from my lesbian friends' point of view), relating to other women sexually. How could they trust someone who slept with a man? I had of course suffered under a variation of this question before—from black people. How could they trust someone who slept with a white person? All such questions reflect the questioner's vulnerability and lack of self-confidence, but few of us recognize this at the time. We are flung into a solitude so severe that it inadvertently increases our sense of freedom as it loosens our bonds to any specific group, whether racial or sexual. Our perception of the limitations of ourselves and of others is sharpened considerably, as is the passion of our self-respect. We begin to see that perhaps all people must be our people, since the various factions of peoplehood to which we "belong" are so very hard to please; and that *we* must be "every person" in any event if we are to assume the absolute largest possible freedom for ourselves. I reached the point with both groups, lesbians and blacks, of just saying: Accept me as I am, with this tendency I have of being able to love everyone, including you, or just don't (expletive) bother me at all. On these terms, I am happy to say, I have regained most of the friends I lost.

It is not the lesbians, however, that one "sees" in San Francisco, but gays. This was one of the most striking things to me when I settled here, with a cast of fictional characters for a new novel in my head, lesbian and straight. Women are always together affectionately. The intense female couple you see on the street could as easily be mother and daughter, sisters, best friends, as lovers. It was the intensity between men that was new and that I liked.

I am writing this now partly as a way of remembering Polk and Castro Streets during the late seventies. How the "last man" and I would always cruise those streets on any outing that took us more than a few blocks from home. At first I thought our interest was simply voyeurism, or maybe my lover was a latent gay (I sometimes wondered); but it was something other and different from that. Neither of us had ever seen men taking such obvious delight in each other (and both our fathers had been physically distant from us and emotionally repressed), and to us their caring seemed to say something delightful about the possibilities of men. To drive slowly up Castro, near the theater, and to be met by the sight of two grown men locked together in a thorough and obviously toe-curling kiss was a revelation. And sometimes they both had mustaches! It was a bit like my seeing a bearded iris for the first time.

Very often there were parades. On Halloween, for several years, we dressed up as various night creatures and trick-or-treated about the city, taking in the fabulous costumes, the outrageous hair styles and make-up only gays would have the queerness to make and the imagination to wear. I loved the life that gays gave Halloween, a holiday I learned to enjoy only because of them; and I was always reassured by the presence of Sister Boom Boom (a gay man) on the electoral ballot, and by pictures of the Sister himself, demure in white scapular and black habit, "nun of the above," making still another bid for Board of Supervisors. There was another side, darker (or whiter) and more sinister. There were gays dressed like Nazis, who frightened me. There were those who seemed enamored of whips and chains. White well-to-do gays who moved into poor black neighborhoods and gentrified them to death, gradually forcing black people out. But there was also something cheering to the soul about these men, all colors, classes, and conditions, who, in spite of everything that had been taught them about the evil of it, steadfastly affirmed their right to love each other. And to be open and frolicsome about it. I came to understand why homosexual men are called "gay." Because they hadn't repressed their basic feelings the way most straight men seem to, they were full of vitality and fun. I could imagine that straight men, who so often appear dead behind the eyes and immobile below the neck, resented them for this. Now I hear on the news that one out of every two gays in San Francisco has AIDS. Many are dying. In this crisis the gay community has shown courage and tenderness equal to its former raunchiness; the city itself has been compassionate and brave. Still, it is rare these days even to see heterosexuals kissing on the street. It is as if we are all mourning the loss of spontaneous outrageousness. I miss the shock, the revelation, the smile evoked by the sight of two people (whatever they are, and even if they're more than two!) brazenly expressing love, or just unmistakable intent.

How sad now never to see men holding hands, while everywhere one looks they are holding guns.

So many cultures have died it is hard to contemplate the

possible loss or dulling over of another one, or to accept the fact that once again those of us who can appreciate all the bearded irises of life will be visually, spiritually, and emotionally deprived.

1987

WHY DID THE BALINESE CHICKEN
CROSS THE ROAD?

"Why do you keep putting off writing about me?" It is the voice of a chicken that asks this. Depending on where you are, you will laugh, or not laugh. Either response is appropriate. The longer I am a writer—so long now that my writing finger is periodically numb—the better I understand what writing is; what its function is; what it is supposed to do. I learn that the writer's pen is a microphone held up to the mouths of ancestors and even stones of long ago. That once given permission by the writer—a fool, and so why should one fear?—horses, dogs, rivers, and, yes, chickens can step forward and expound on their lives. The magic of this is not so much in the power of the microphone as in the ability of the nonhuman object or animal to *be* and the human animal to *perceive its being*.

This then is about a chicken I knew in Bali. I do not know her name or that of her parents and grandparents. I do not know where she was from originally. Suddenly on a day whose morning had been rainy, there she was, on the path in front of us (my own family, on our way back to our temporary shelter), trying to look for worms, trying to point out other possible food items to her three chicks, and trying at the same time to get herself and her young ones across the road.

It is one of those moments that will be engraved on my brain forever. For I really *saw* her. She was small and gray, flecked with black; so were her chicks. She had a healthy red comb and quick, light-brown eyes. She was that proud, chunky chicken shape that makes one feel always that chickens, and hens especially, have personality and *will*. Her steps were neat and quick and authoritative; and though she never touched her chicks, it was obvious she was shepherding them along. She clucked impatiently when, our feet falling ever nearer, one of them, especially self-absorbed and perhaps hard-headed, ceased to respond.

When my friend Joanne—also one of my editors at *Ms.* magazine for nearly fifteen years—knew I was going to Bali, she asked if I would consider writing about it. There was so much there to write about, after all: the beautiful Balinese, the spectacular countryside, the ancient myths, dances, and rituals; the food, the flowers, the fauna, too. When I returned, with no word on Bali, she asked again. I did not know how to tell her that my strongest experience on Bali had been to really be able to see, and identify with, a chicken. Joanne probably eats chicken, I thought.

I did, too.

In fact, just before going to Bali I had been fasting, drinking juices only, and wondering if I could give up the eating of meat. I had even been looking about in San Francisco for an animal rights organization to join (though it is the animal liberationists, who set animals free, who actually take my heart); in that way I hoped to meet others of my kind, i.e., those who are beginning to feel, or have always felt, that eating meat is cannibalism. On the day my companion pointed out such an organization, in an Australian magazine we found at a restaurant in Ubud, I was slow to speak, because I had a delicious piece of Balinese-style chicken satay in my mouth.

I have faced the distressing possibility that I may never be a "pure" vegetarian. There is the occasional stray drumstick or slice of prosciutto that somehow finds its way into my mouth, even though purchased meat no longer appears in my kitchen. Since Bali, nearly a year ago, I have eaten several large pieces of Georgia ham (a cherished delicacy from my childhood, as is fried chicken; it is hard to consider oneself Southern without it!) and several pieces of chicken prepared by a long-lost African friend from twenty years ago who, while visiting, tired of my incessant chopping of vegetables to stir-fry and eat over rice and therefore cooked a chicken and served it in protest. There have been three crab dinners and even one of shrimp.

I console myself by recognizing that this diet, in which ninety percent of what I eat is nonmeat and nondairy, though not pristinely vegetarian, is still completely different from and less barbarous than the one I was raised on—in which meat was a mainstay—and that perhaps if they knew or cared (and somehow I know they know and care), my chicken and fish sister/fellow travelers on the planet might give me credit for effort.

I wonder.

Perhaps I will win this struggle, too, though. I can never *not* know that the chicken I absolutely *saw* is a sister (this recognition gives a whole different meaning to the expression "you chicks"), and that her love of her children definitely resembles my love of mine. Sometimes I cast my quandary about it all in the form of a philosophical chicken joke: Why did the Balinese chicken cross the road? I know the answer is, To try to get both of us to the other side.

It is not so much a question of whether the lion will one day lie down with the lamb, but whether human beings will ever be able to lie down with any creature or being at all.

1987

. . . .

JOURNAL

June 17, 1987

Early this morning; as I was putting the finishing touches on this book, I received an urgent call from "Liz" of Neighbor to Neighbor, an activist group that successfully gets out news about the wars in Central America, using U.S. media, primarily television. Two days from now there will be a program it has organized called "The Peace Oscars"—named for Archbishop Oscar Romero, who was a defender of poor people's rights in El Salvador until his assassination, by an agent of the Salvadoran government, while he administered mass in his church. At the ceremony, which will be held in the beautiful Conservatory of Flowers in Golden Gate Park in San Francisco, six of the bravest and most compassionate of human beings will be honored: people who have risked their lives to take medicine, food, clothing, and technical skills to the poor and suffering people of Central America; men and women who have been arrested

many times as they exercised their opposition to the often gen-
ocidal policies of the U.S. government; people who founded
the Sanctuary Movement in this country; one refugee woman
from El Salvador, whose personal story of oppression, terror,
escape, and commitment, told at hundreds of gatherings in the
United States, radicalized the people who heard her and deep-
ened their commitment to the struggle to end war. I am to co-
host this program, and, in fact, give the Peace Oscar (a small
blue ceramic bird) to the sister from El Salvador.

The urgent message from Liz, however, is that a bomb
threat against the ceremony has been telephoned by a mechan-
ical-sounding male voice that said our crime is that we do not
want to fight communism. Because several of the participants
and invited guests are federally appointed officials of the state
of California, she tells me, there will be federal agents about,
cordons of police and various SWAT teams, whose job it will
be to sweep the place clean of any bombs. This often happens
to movements like ours, she sighs. She tells me everyone in-
volved will be called, in order for each to decide whether to
come or stay home.

Of course I remember bomb threats, and bombs, from the
sixties. I think of the children, Angela Davis's young acquaint-
ances, blown up while in Sunday school. I think of Ralph
Featherstone, a SNCC worker, blown up in his car. I think of
the NAACP official, who, along with his wife, was blown up
while in bed. When I lived in Mississippi, bombings occurred;
when my husband and I moved there, the bombing/lynching
of NAACP leader Vernon Dehmer was in the news. I remember
the bombing of Dr. Martin Luther King's house. There is a
long history of bombings in North America. This is not the first
time "communism" has been used as an excuse.

I send along the message of the threat to the people I've
invited. But I know I will not be deterred. I spend a few hours

with my lawyer and finally draw up my overdue will and assign a durable power of attorney that will be effective through the weekend (the affair is to take place on a Friday night). It isn't fatalism, or courage; I simply can't imagine not being there to honor these amazing, but also ordinary, people. I can't imagine not being there to hug my sister from the south.

A writer, apparently, to the core (though I frequently kid myself that if I never write again it's fine with me; there's so much else to do—sitting in a rocking chair watching the ocean, for instance), I find my thoughts going to my unfinished manuscripts. If anything happened to me, I wonder what my editor, John the meticulous, could make of my unfinished novel, a third typed and in a drawer, a third typed and in the computer, a third in my notebook and head.

What of this book? I realize that, as it stands, it has the rounded neatness of contemplation, and I would like to leave the reader with the uneven (I almost said ragged) edge of activity. I returned to my notes for the past week, and this is what I found:

I am Nicaraguan; I am Salvadoran; I am Grenadian; I am Caribbean; and I am Central American.

For the past several days I have been thinking about this sentence, and wondering what I mean by it. I am also Norte Americana, an African-American, even an African-Indian-Gringo American, if I add up all the known elements of my racial composition (and include the white rapist grandfather). Perhaps this is one way that I am Nicaraguan, or Salvadoran, or Grenadian. For the people in those countries, too, are racially mixed; in their country, too, there are the reds, the blacks, the whites—and the browns.

But I think the primary reason that I feel so Central American/Caribbean is that when I look at those people—and even though I study but do not yet speak their language—I see myself.

I see my family, I see my parents, I see the ancestors. When I look at Nicaraguans, at, for instance, the humble peasant woman being "interrogated" by a Contra carrying several guns and knives and three times her size, when I see and identify with her terror, when I look at the vulnerable faces of the nearly naked and barefoot children, when I see the suffering and pain on the faces of the men, then I am seeing a great deal of my own life.

I, too, was born poor, in an impoverished part of the world. I was born on what had been a plantation in the South, in Georgia. My parents and grandparents worked hard all their lives for barely enough food and shelter to sustain them. They were sharecroppers—landless peasants—the product of whose labor was routinely stolen from them. Their parents and grandparents were enslaved. To me, Central America is one large plantation; and I see the people's struggle to be free as a slave revolt.

I can remember in my own life the days of *injusticia* that continue in so much of the world today. The days when children withered in sickness and disease (as I have withered) because there was no money to pay for their care and no concern for their health anyway, by the larger society. I myself have suffered the deprivations of poverty, so that when I look into the face of a Central American peasant, a Caribbean peasant, I see myself.

And I remember the years of fighting the white bosses of Georgia, Alabama, and Mississippi, especially, and of occasionally winning our battles for dignity and bread against them—though at a cost (so many of the people we loved were brutalized or assassinated) that still bruises the heart. When I see the proud though weary faces of the Sandinistas, I see our own young faces. The faces that went south in the sixties to teach black people to read and write, to go out to vote, to stand up and be counted. And to keep the eyes on the prize.

It is the same spirit. The spirit of poor people who have

been ground down nearly to a fine powder of humanity and yet who stand like rocks and refuse to be blown away.

I am Nicaraguan. I am Salvadoran. I am Grenadian, Honduran, I chant to myself. It has almost become a mantra.

And yet, this year I paid more in taxes than my parents and grandparents together earned all the years they worked the land of the gringos of the South. And over half of that money will go to buy weapons that will be shipped from the Concord Naval Weapons Station at Port Chicago, California, thirty miles from my home, and used against these people that I think of as myself.

These were my thoughts a few days before I was arrested for blocking one of the gates to the Concord Naval Weapons Station.

It was a hot, dusty day, June 12, 1987, and I woke up thinking of all the things I needed to bring to the demonstration: a hat, sunblock, drinking water, food, spare clothing (in case we were in jail for longer than a day), whatever medical supplies I might need. I drove to the weapons station with the three other members of my affinity group: Robert, Belvie, and Paul. Belvie and I had designed beautiful turquoise-and-coral T-shirts with the name of our group (Wild Trees), a large mushroom cloud, and the words "Remember Port Chicago."

For the past ten years I have shared my life with the writer and sometimes political activist (primarily in the Civil Rights movement and against the Vietnam War) Robert Allen, who all that time has been writing a book about the so-called accident at Port Chicago on July 17, 1944. What happened was that 320 men whose job it was to load the bombs being sent to use on Japan and other places in the Pacific were blown to bits (literally), along with the ships they were loading and much of the base and nearby town. Two hundred of those killed were black.

Because theirs had been the job of loading the weapons onto the ships, theirs was also the job of picking up the pieces—of men and debris—left by the explosion. When asked to continue loading the bombs after this horrendous experience, most of the men said no. They were threatened, imprisoned, tried for mutiny. Sentenced. Sent to jail. Released years later with dishonorable discharges.

My friend Robert has tracked down many of the surviving "mutineers" and, over the years, continued to wrestle with the implications of this event for America.

Port Chicago is now Concord. The name has been changed and the old town of Port Chicago completely destroyed, razed, in fact, by the government. But the weapons remain. Rather, they remain long enough to be shipped out—to Japan (the bomb dropped on Hiroshima was shipped from here), Vietnam, Nicaragua, and now El Salvador.

A few days before the demonstration we—the organizers (The Pledge of Resistance), the news media, demonstrators-to-be, and I—stood on a hill overlooking the base. We could see the white trains—white to reflect the heat—going into bunkers built into the hillside. Inside those bunkers are some of the deadliest weapons ever devised. There is, for instance, something that sounds even worse than napalm: the white phosphorous rocket. The sparks from it burn through the skin and flesh and into the bone. It can take a week for the burning to be put out. I have seen photographs of children who have lost limbs to the sparks from this rocket. I have found unbearable the suffering and questions in their eyes.

The morning of the demonstration I dress in jeans, sneakers, sunglasses, and an old felt hat, and I carry with me a sweet-faced black doll with crisp, shiny hair. I've named her Windela after a newborn niece of the same name I have not yet seen, and because I want to symbolize the connection I feel to Winnie and Nelson Mandela and the common awareness that it is up to those of us who are adults to leave to all children a habitable planet.

During the previous week I have felt afraid. I have hardly been able to smile at anyone. Though I have risked arrest many times, while a student demonstrator at Spelman College, in Liberty County, Georgia, and in Mississippi as a civil rights worker, I have been arrested only once before, during a demonstration against apartheid at UC, Berkeley. I felt a light-hearted joy throughout that action; as I sat with other demonstrators I could not suppress smiles *and* song. I concluded that what was different this time was that I would be placing myself in such vulnerable proximity to an enormous pile of evil and death blandly passed off to motorists, who can actually see the trains and bunkers from the highway, as bucolic countryside: cows graze placidly in the grass about the bunkers, giving them the aspect of odd kinds of barns.

Still, as I filled my backpack with a toothbrush, aspirin, and fruit, I began to take heart, the image of the children, the trees, and the animals of the planet always before me. On arrival, we went immediately to the gate to be blocked. There were a few protesters, about a hundred, already there. Across a broad yellow line, soldiers dressed in helmets and camouflage fatigues stood spread-legged holding long riot sticks. Behind them stood a row of officers in khaki from the local sheriff's department. Behind them another row of officers, presumably a SWAT team, in navy blue. The four of us walked up to face the soldiers, who were staring straight ahead. Between their row and that of the officers from the sheriff's department stood a Catholic priest, a woman in her fifties, and two old people, a man and a woman. They were all white. It was then that I made an interesting observation: Aside from myself and two members of our affinity group, there were no other people of color there. The Army, represented by the soldiers standing in front of us, was much more integrated. *Merde!* I thought. What does it mean, that the forces of destruction are more integrated than the forces of peace?

Almost at once a white car carrying an official of the base arrived at the gate. We turned to face it, not permitting it to go through. The driver consulted with an Army officer, and the car slowly pulled away. Another and another vehicle appeared. They were not admitted. Soon a woman drove up and said she needed to fill a prescription at the base; it was spontaneously agreed that she should be let through. Many of us walked behind her car to close the space behind her. Soon a man who said he had gout and was coming to see his doctor appeared. He was also let through. A woman next to me said that in anticipation of our blockade the weapons trains and trucks had been busy all night long.

We were arrested because we went through the line of soldiers—all of them mere children and obviously poor (bad skin, crooked teeth, a certain ghetto street-corner patina)—and stood with the priest and the woman in her fifties, and the two old people. The old woman, Teresa, with a wondrously wrinkled face and bright white hair (a true crone), clasped me to her thin chest. The old man, Abraham (yes), half Jewish and half American Indian, looked fixedly into the crowd behind us and sang a frail but steady version of "Amen." I felt very proud of our affinity group. Of Robert, who had joined this inner group first, of Paul, who had promptly followed, and of Belvie, who was now smiling and talking to Teresa as if they were old friends.

A lot of things went through my mind as I was being handcuffed. Would they take my doll, whom I'd managed to stuff under one arm? No, they did not. Had my statements to the press truly reflected my feelings about weapons and war? I had been asked why I was risking arrest and I had said because

I can't stand knowing that the money I pay in taxes and that my own family needs—not to mention all the other poor and sick people in this country and world—pays for weapons and the policy that maims, kills, frightens, and horribly abuses babies, children, women, men, and the old. I don't want to be a murderer, I had said.

And once, as I was being lifted into the jail van, someone yelled, "What do you have to say now, as you go off to jail?" and I made a joke that was the truth: "I'm following my tax dollars," I said.

My tax dollars. Really the crux of the matter. When will I have the courage not to pay them? I remember being audited by the IRS when my husband and I were in the Civil Rights movement in Mississippi. I remember being audited here in California two years ago. It isn't so much courage that I would need, as the patience to endure the grinding malice of bureaucratic harassment. (Meanwhile, my letter to my congressman about implementation of a peace tax—a peace tax would go to build hospitals, schools, houses, and to provide food for people—has not been answered.)

My thoughts, while I was being frisked, fingerprinted, and photographed (I liked my mug shot) by very cordial men and women, some of whom admired my doll, turned to food. Of which, because I'd left my well-provisioned backpack in the car, I had none. As a vegetarian, which I've now been for a good three months, I get hungry frequently. I think about oranges, almonds, apples—and, yes, a well-cooked piece of chicken. As soon as I'm seated fairly comfortably in the holding area—a large gray "cattle car" from the Port Chicago explosion days— Sallie, the woman in her fifties, breaks out her stash of oranges, Swiss cheese, and Triscuits, and offers me some. I think about how hard it would be for me to engage in any kind of action now for justice and peace with the remains of murdered flesh in my body. I'm tempted to wonder about the cows who "gave" the "Swiss" cheese, but don't. I eat it with gratitude.

Apparently it is lunchtime for everyone. I look out the window of our cattle car and I see that the guards, the nurse, the people who checked us in (even the one black woman in a light-blue uniform, who asked for my autograph and said, "Oh, I'm so glad you're here!"), all are eating. Since this is California, they are eating thick whole-grain sandwiches fluffy with fillings, trailing juicy tomato slices, lettuce leaves, and sprouts. As we all munch, they outside and "free," me inside and "captive," I can't help a feeling of tenderness for them: the need to eat connects us. Perhaps that is why they have taken these jobs.

Though some of our demonstrators were brutalized by the police, we were not. In an effort to minimize the import of our action, the meaning of it, and to keep public anxiety about the close proximity of the nuclear weapons on the base as low as possible, they treated us, for the most part, courteously. In truth, many of them seemed bored, barely present in what they were doing. There are some demonstrators who feel it is best, as far as gaining publicity is concerned, to have at least some police brutality, but I am not one of those. The pictures of demonstrations that I like show the creativity as well as the determination of the crowd. I like costumes, slogans, effigies. I think if these things are true enough, the police can affirm them, too. The most encouraging demonstration picture I've seen recently is of a young Korean policeman, visor raised and shield lowered, smiling impishly at protesting students and giving them the victory sign. Of course, many policemen are brutal and take their position as guardians of the status quo seriously. Many of them are angry, because they feel they are poor and have to work while the demonstrators appear to be playing. I feel absolutely no anger toward the police just because they are police or toward the young men in the Army. The protection of evil must be the most self-destructive job of all.

The next day, freed, my doll Windela and I address a crowd of a thousand demonstrators, two hundred of whom will later be arrested. Among other things, I read a poem about a poor Salvadoran woman whose father, husband, and sons have been killed and whose remaining small children are starving; nevertheless she is paying her taxes. Later, I stand holding Windela beside the knee-high, coiled line of razor-blade wire, on the other side of which are the same young black, white, brown, and yellow recruits. They are, at the moment, receiving much shouted information from several huge Vietnam vets, so loud and intense they frighten me—"Why do you want to go fight their stupid war for them, huh?" "Here's a body bag"—*plop*—"do you want to come back in one of those?" "I swore when I was in Nam that if I ever got out alive I'd never sit back and let kids like you go!" As I stand there, I suddenly feel a small stroking along my thigh. I look down into the large brown eyes of a small, gentle-faced olive-brown girl. She is playing shyly with Windela's foot. I hand the doll to her, and she embraces it with joy. Beside her is her mother, holding an infant. She speaks to the little girl in Spanish. I ask the mother, who appears to be in her early twenties, where she is from. She tells me she is a refugee from El Salvador, that she lives in a refugee house in San Francisco. At some point in our halting conversation in her "leetle beet" of English and my truly tongue-tied smidgen of Spanish, I ask to hold the baby, a plump, six-month-old girl, who promptly yanks off one of my earrings and then, fortunately, has trouble finding her mouth. Her mother says she is looking for a job. Can I help her? I tell her I will try. But who will hire a young mother of two small children who speaks Spanish?

I leave the doll with her daughter, Sandra, last seen sitting on the ground, oblivious to the demonstrators, the arrests, the police, and the Army all around her, "being a mother." And yes, that is what motherhood more and more is like in this world. I am glad I have acted. Glad I am here, if only for her. She is the future. I want some of the best of me, of us, of this day, to go there with her.

September 1, 1987
Today Belvie called to tell me the news about Brian Willson. He was blocking the tracks at the Concord Naval Weapons Station, along with several others, and the train ran over him, injuring his head and left ankle, and severing his right leg below the knee. He had been in a peace circle earlier in the morning with our friend Dan, whom I called immediately. Dan told me that in fact, in addition to the head injuries, which he thought very grave, and the severed right leg, Brian's left foot and ankle had been crushed, so that leg, too, below the knee, was amputated. As he talks, I feel a flush of futility that this could happen, although we've all realized it could, and, already thinking of what Brian's life will be like without the use of his legs, I can barely absorb the information Dan is giving me. Apparently the train speeded up when the demonstrators were spotted. Moments before the attack, Brian, who was preparing for a forty-day fast and sit-in on the tracks, and who had been married eight days before, had said he was willing to give his life to the struggle for peace.

Brian. White, middle-aged, wonderfully warm and expressive brown eyes (lots of light), brown hair, with some gray, a mottled beard. A really lovely and intelligent smile (how would he smile now?)—and great legs.

We met at the planning of the original blockade of the weapons station, and I had liked him right away. A week later we were together, with hundreds of others, blockading the gates. Only later did I learn he'd been an Air Force officer during the Vietnam War, in intelligence, no less. I could see how sick he was of war, and of the lies that protect war. He spoke very quietly but with a knowledge of what we were up against, so often missing in those who wage peace. He had the aura of someone who had seen and had enough.

I remember him telling us that if the death trains got through our blockade and over our bodies, killing or maiming us, we should realize that when their weapons reached their destinations, in Nicaragua or El Salvador, this would also be the fate of the people there. We are not more than they, he said; they are not less than we. The weapons on the trains would maim and kill children, women, and men, he said. To which I mentally added animals, trees, rivers, families, communities, cultures, friendship, love—and our own self-respect.

> Whoever you are
> whatever you are
> start with that,
> whether salt
> of the earth
> or only
> white sugar.

. . . .

THE UNIVERSE RESPONDS:

OR, HOW I LEARNED WE CAN HAVE

PEACE ON EARTH

To some people who read the following there will seem to be something special or perhaps strange about me. I have sometimes felt this way myself. To others, however, what I am about to write will appear obvious. I think our response to "strangeness" or "specialness" depends on where we are born, where we are raised, how much idle time we have had to watch trees (long enough at least to notice there is not an ugly one among them) swaying in the wind. Or to watch rivers, rainstorms, or the sea.

A few years ago, I wrote an essay called "Everything Is a Human Being," which explores to some extent the Native American view that all of creation is of one substance and therefore deserving of the same respect. I described the death of a snake that I caused and wrote of my remorse. I wrote the piece to celebrate the birth of Martin Luther King, Jr., and I read it first to a large group of college students in California. I also read it other places, so that by summer (I had written it in winter) it had been read three or four times, and because I cannot bear to repeat myself very much, I put it away.

That summer "my" land in the country crawled with snakes. There was always the large resident snake, whom my mother named "Susie," crawling about in the area that marks the entrance to my studio. But there were also lots of others wherever we looked. A black-and-white king snake appeared underneath the shower stall in the garden. A striped red-and-black one, very pretty, appeared near the pond. It now revealed the little hole in the ground in which it lived by lying half in and half out of it as it basked in the sun. Garden snakes crawled up and down the roads and paths. One day, leaving my house with a box of books in his arms, my companion literally tripped over one of these.

We spoke to all these snakes in friendly voices. They went their way. We went ours. After about a two-week bloom of snakes, we seemed to have our usual number: just Susie and a couple of her children.

A few years later, I wrote an essay about a horse called Blue. It was about how humans treat horses and other animals; how hard it is for us to see them as the suffering, fully conscious, enslaved beings they are. It also marked the beginning of my effort to become non-meat-eating (fairly successful). After reading this essay in public only once, this is what happened. A white horse came and settled herself on the land. (Her owner, a neighbor, soon came to move her.) The two horses on the ranch across the road began to run up to their fence whenever I passed, leaning over it and making what sounded to my ears like joyful noises. They had never done this before (I checked with the human beings I lived with to be sure of this), and after a few more times of greeting me as if I'd done something especially nice for them, they stopped. Now when I pass they look at me with the same reserve they did before. But there is still a spark of *recognition*.

What to make of this?

What I have noticed in my small world is that if I praise the wild flowers growing on the hill in front of my house, the following year they double in profusion and brilliance. If I admire the squirrel that swings from branch to branch outside my window, pretty soon I have three or four squirrels to admire. If I look into the eyes of a raccoon that has awakened me by noisily rummaging through the garbage at night, and acknowledge that it looks maddeningly like a mischievous person—paws on hips, masked eyes, a certain impudent stance, as it looks back at me—I soon have a family of raccoons living in a tree a few yards off my deck. (From this tree they easily forage in the orchard at night and eat, or at least take bites out of, all the apples. Which is not fun. But that is another story.)

And then, too, there are the deer, who know they need never, ever fear me.

In white-directed movies about the Indians of the Old West, you sometimes see the "Indians" doing a rain dance, a means of praying for rain. The message delivered by the moviemaker is that such dancing and praying is ridiculous, that either it will rain or it will not. All white men know this. The Indians are backward and stupid and wasting their time. But there is also that last page or so in the story of Black Elk, in which his anthropologist/friend John Neihardt goes with him on a last visit to the Badlands to pray atop Horney Peak, a place sacred to the Sioux. It is a cloudless day, but the ancient Black Elk hopes that the Great Spirit, as in the real "old" days, will acknowledge his prayer for the good of his people by sending at least a few drops of rain. As he prays, in his old, tired voice, mostly of his love of the Universe and his failure to be perfect, a small cloud indeed forms. It rains, just enough to say "Yes." Then the sky clears. Even today there is the belief among many indigenous holy people that when a person of goodness dies, the Universe acknowledges the spirit's departure by sending storms and rain.

The truth is, in the country, where I live much of the time, I am virtually overrun by birds and animals—raccoons, snakes, deer, horses (occasionally). During a recent court trial at which a neighbor and I both happened to find ourselves, her opening words of greeting included the information that two wild pigs she'd somehow captured had broken out and were, she feared, holed up somewhere on my land.

But at least, I thought, my house in the city is safe.

But no.

One night after dinner, as some friends were leaving my house, I opened my front door, only to have a large black dog walk gratefully inside. It had obviously been waiting quietly on the stoop. It came into the hallway, sniffed my hands, and prepared to make itself at home, exactly as if it had lived in my house all its life. There was no nervousness whatsoever about being an intruder. No, no, I said, out you go! It did not want to go, but my friends and I persuaded it. It settled itself at the door and there it stayed, barking reproachfully until I went to bed. Very late that night I heard its owners calling it. George! they called. George! Here, George! They were cursing and laughing. Drunk. George made no response.

I suddenly realized that George was not lost. He had run away. He had run away from these cursing, laughing drunks who were now trying to find him. This realization meant the end of sleep for me that night as I lay awake considering my responsibility to George. (I felt none toward his owners.) For George obviously "knew" which house was at least *supposed* to be a stop on the underground railroad, and had come to it; but I, in my city house, had refused to acknowledge my house as such. If I let it in, where would I put it? Then, too, I'm not particularly fond of the restlessness of dogs. The way they groan and fart in their sleep, chase rabbits in their dreams, and flop themselves over, rattling their chains (i.e., collars and dog tags). George had run away from these drunks who "owned" him, people no doubt unfit to own anything at all that breathed. Did they beat him? Did they tie him to trees and lampposts outside pubs (as I've so often seen done) while they went inside and had drink after drink? Were all the "lost" dogs one heard about really runaways? It hit me with great force that a dog I had once had, Myshkin, had undoubtedly run away from the small enclosed backyard in which he had been kept and in which he was probably going mad, whereas I had for years indulged in the fantasy that he'd been stolen! No dog in his right mind would voluntarily leave a cushy prison run by loving humans, right?

Or suppose George was a woman, beaten or psychologically abused by her spouse. What then? Would I let her in? I would, wouldn't I? But where to put George, anyway? If I put him in the cellar, he might bark. I hate the sound of barking. If I put him in the parlor, he might spread fleas. Who was this dog, anyway?

George stayed at my door the whole night. In the morning I heard him bark, but by the time I was up, he was gone.

I think I am telling you that the animals of the planet are in desperate peril, and that they are fully aware of this. No less than human beings are doing in all parts of the world, they are seeking sanctuary. But I am also telling you that we are connected to them at least as intimately as we are connected to trees. Without plant life human beings could not breathe. Plants produce oxygen. Without free animal life I believe we will lose the spiritual equivalent of oxygen. "Magic," intuition, sheer astonishment at the forms the Universe devises in which to express life—itself—will no longer be able to breathe in us. One day it occurred to me that if all the birds died, as they might well do, eventually, from the poisoning of their air, water, and food, it would be next to impossible to describe to our children the wonder of their flight. To most children, I think, the flight of a bird—if they'd never seen one fly—would be imagined as stiff and unplayful, like the flight of an airplane.

But what I'm also sharing with you is this thought: The Universe responds. What you ask of it, it gives. The military-industrial complex and its leaders and scientists have shown more faith in this reality than have those of us who do not believe in war and who want peace. They have asked the Earth for all its deadlier substances. They have been confident in their faith in hatred and war. The Universe, ever responsive, the Earth, ever giving, has opened itself fully to their desires. Ironically, Black Elk and nuclear scientists can be viewed in much the same way: as men who prayed to the Universe for what they believed they needed and who received from it a sign reflective of their own hearts.

I remember when I used to dismiss the bumper sticker "Pray for Peace." I realize now that I did not understand it, since I also did not understand prayer; which I know now to be the active affirmation in the physical world of our inseparableness from the divine; and everything, *especially* the physical world, is divine. War will stop when we no longer praise it, or give it any attention at all. Peace will come wherever it is sincerely invited. Love will overflow every sanctuary given it. Truth will grow where the fertilizer that nourishes it is also truth. Faith will be its own reward.

Believing this, which I learned from my experience with the animals and the wild flowers, I have found that my fear of nuclear destruction has been to a degree lessened. I know perfectly well that we may all die, and relatively soon, in a global holocaust, which was first imprinted, probably against their wishes, on the hearts of the scientist fathers of the atomic bomb, no doubt deeply wounded and frightened human beings; but I also know we have the power, as all the Earth's people, to conjure up the healing rain imprinted on Black Elk's heart. Our death is in our hands.

Knock and the door shall be opened. Ask and you shall receive.

Whatsoever you do the least of these, you do also unto me—and to yourself. For we are one.

"God" answers prayers. Which is another way of saying, "the Universe responds."

We are *indeed* the world. Only if we have reason to fear what is in our own hearts need we fear for the planet. Teach yourself peace.

Pass it on.

1987

PUBLICATION

ACKNOWLEDGMENTS

• • • • • • • • •

"Am I Blue?": *Ms.*, July 1986.

"Father": *Essence* (as "Father for What You Were"), May 1985.

"The Dummy in the Window: Joel Chandler Harris and the Invention of Uncle Remus": *Southern Exposure* 9 (as "Uncle Remus, No Friend of Mine"), Summer 1981.

"Longing to Die of Old Age": *Ms.* (as "On Excellence: America Should Have Closed Down When . . ."), January 1985.

"Journal, August 1984": *Sage*, Spring 1985.

"Coming In from the Cold": *Ms.* (As "Finding Celie's Voice"), December 1985.

"Oppressed Hair Puts a Ceiling on the Brain": *Spelman Messenger*, Summer 1987.

"In the Closet of the Soul": *Ms.*, November 1986.

"A Name Is Sometimes an Ancestor Saying Hi, I'm with You": *Sojourners*, (as "She Smiles Within My Smile"), December 1986.

"A Thousand Words: A Writer's Pictures of China": *Ms.* (as "China: A Poet Takes Snapshots in Her Mind"), March 1985.

"Journey to Nine Miles": *Mother Jones* (As "Redemption Day"), December 1986.

"My Daughter Smokes": *In These Times* (as "Slavery on Tobacco Road"), March 1987.

"On *Seeing Red*": *Socialist Review*, March-April 1984.

"Not Only Will Your Teachers Appear, They Will Cook New Foods for You": *Mendocino Country*, Issue 52, September 1, 1986.

"Everything Is a Human Being": *Ms.* (as "When a Tree Falls: Alice Walker on the Future of the Planet"), January 1984.

" 'Nobody Was Supposed to Survive' ": *In These Times*, December 17–23, 1986.

"Why Did the Balinese Chicken Cross the Road?": *Woman of Power*, February 1988.

"The Universe Responds": *Spelman Messenger*, Summer 1987.